Science Investigations for
Elementary School Teachers

Science Investigations for Elementary School Teachers

Kenneth D. George
University of Pennsylvania

Maureen A. Dietz
University of Maryland

Eugene C. Abraham
Temple University

D. C. HEATH AND COMPANY
Lexington, Massachusetts Toronto London

Published simultaneously in Canada.

Printed in the United States of America

International Standard Book Number: 0-669-83154-9

Library of Congress Catalog Card Number: 73-2555

Contents

v

Introduction

During the past decade, the curriculum offerings of the schools of the United States have been examined critically. The science curricula received the greatest scrutiny, especially in the area of the objectives and the teaching methods used to attain these objectives. One finding was that science textbooks were organized around a body of knowledge. Another was that these texts were read by the students, who memorized the facts and repeated them on examinations. Another result of this scrutiny was that teachers viewed their role as presenting the facts from the textbooks through lectures or class discussions, the major objective being to complete the textbook during the school year.

Educators and scientists realized that such methods presented science as only a body of knowledge; therefore, curricula and textbooks based on that definition and teaching methods stressing the importance of acquiring vast numbers of facts could not be justified. They reasoned that science is not just a body of knowledge, but includes *the methods used to generate, organize, and evaluate that knowledge.* Such a view has important implications for the teaching of science.

Teaching Techniques There are two techniques that are commonly used in teaching elementary school science: (1) didactic teaching, which is under the control and direction of the teacher, book, or curriculum; and (2) inquiry teaching, where the learner generates knowledge by himself. In most classrooms, science is taught didactically. Children do not ask questions, or if they do, they are not permitted or encouraged to find out the answers on their own. The answers or conclusions to problems are given to the children by the teacher or the textbook. The teacher assumes that the children will accept all that he teaches as fact and will look to him or the book as the provider of the answers to questions.

Though it may be defined in many ways, we have defined inquiry as *that mode of learning whereby the learner uses skills and attitudes to generate, organize, and evaluate knowledge.* This definition is quite similar to the definition of science presented above. This view of learning does not put major emphasis on the accumulation of facts, but it does on the use of skills and attitudes that are necessary for the children to inquire into science. Inquiry helps children find answers to problems that arise in their lives, just as these problems arise in the explorations of scientists. Children will not always be students in a classroom, but they will be living in a world that presents many problems, and each child will be required to make his own unique response to these problems.

We firmly believe that most teachers would prefer to use inquiry teaching techniques in their classrooms. However, they just don't know how because they have rarely learned through inquiry themselves. We hope that the investigations in this book will help teachers to help the children in their classrooms acquire the skills and attitudes necessary to learn through inquiry.

Inquiry Teaching Just as reading is a fundamental method for exploring whatever may be written, so inquiry is a fundamental method for exploring whatever may be tested by observation and experimentation in science, which is more than a body of facts, a collection of principles, and a set of instruments for measurement. Science is a way of asking and answering questions. It is easy to teach a child the facts of science; it is more difficult to teach him these facts in relation to the process of inquiry. The intellectual gain is far greater than the child's ability to conduct a chemical experiment or to name some of the characteristics of static electricity. The child who learns through inquiry will approach the claims of authority with the same spirit of alert skepticism that he adopts toward scientific theories. It is here that the future citizen will learn that science is not memory or magic, but rather a disciplined form of human curiosity.

As a part of the inquiry process, children should be able to evaluate their work and work with others in planning an investigation. They should listen to others, participate in group discussions, manipulate equipment, read, apply previously learned concepts and principles to interpret new phenomena, develop a vocabulary to describe phenomena, and keep records of their work.

The skills and attitudes of science can be developed when children are given the opportunity to participate actively in the learning process. Children must be encouraged to develop a curiosity about the world; to look at things open-mindedly; to be willing to avoid making decisions until as much evidence as possible has been collected; and to change their minds if new evidence is found. Children must be willing to allow others to challenge and question their ideas and to respect others for their ideas. They must be unwilling to accept statements as facts unless they are backed by sufficient evidence. They must be careful not to allow decisions to be affected by personal likes, dislikes, anger, fear, or ignorance. Children should develop an appreciation for the ways science can be used to describe our environment, the influence of science on man's way of thinking and our civilization, the beauty of nature, and the contributions scientists have made.

Probably less needs to be written about the importance of content, as compared with skills and attitudes, since traditionally emphasis in the science classroom has been placed on content, which encompasses the facts, concepts, principles, and conceptual schemes. The content acquired by children will be used in situations other than those in which it was first encountered. In order to accomplish this, the content of science needs to be resistant to forgetting. This can be accomplished through inquiry, which helps to organize it in the learner's mind around conceptual schemes.

Conceptual schemes of science help to pull together the facts, concepts, and principles so that they make sense to the learner. The conceptual schemes help to give meaning to science. The facts, concepts, and principles are no longer separate entities, but their relationship to each other becomes clear. The conceptual schemes bind the sciences together. Even though conceptual schemes may differ with each learner, we have grouped the various investigations in this book under five conceptual schemes of science. Following are the conceptual schemes used in this book:

1. Matter and energy interact between living organisms and their environment.
2. Matter can be measured in mathematical units and these units exist in orderly systems.
3. Changes in matter require energy and the totality of matter and energy is conserved.
4. Living organisms are a product of heredity and environment.
5. The physical universe, and all systems in it, are constantly changing.

The Inquiry Process   When the child sees some phenomena that confuse him, the inquiry process begins. This confusion is caused by an inconsistency in what the child perceives as happening and what he believes should be happening. In order to resolve the inconsistency that has developed, the child needs information. In a didactic classroom, the teacher would resolve the inconsistency by answering the child's question or by directing him to a book.

In an inquiring classroom, the student would resolve the inconsistency with a minimum amount of help from the teacher. To do this the child needs information, which can be obtained by observing, measuring, comparing, and identifying components in the environment. As the child observes, measures, compares, and identifies, he may have to use certain tools, such as a ruler, microscope, or some other piece of equipment. The child must be taught how to use these tools, that is, he must develop psychomotor skills. Even after collecting all this information, the child will still have the inconsistency unless the information obtained makes sense to him.

To make sense out of the data, the child may begin by classifying it. The child may then find he needs to make more observations; this does not imply that the information collected is correct, but only that more information is being collected. Once the child feels he has collected sufficient observations and classified these data, he may then make an inference about the inconsistency; in other words, he attempts to explain the inconsistency. It is with the skill of inferring that the Einsteins and Darwins excelled. Many people can see an inconsistency and collect data, but it is only a few who can recognize some salient feature that the others have missed. However, with practice, each individual may be given the skills necessary to resolve inconsistencies.

The child then formulates hypotheses to explain an inconsistency. These hypotheses are tested and may be eliminated and new ones formulated on the basis of these tests. The number of hypotheses may even be reduced to one. If extensive testing, through controlled experimentation, proves the hypotheses false, the learner may have to collect more data. Once having accepted an hypothesis, the child is capable of making and verifying predictions.

There is no particular order for developing or using these skills of inquiry; however, some or all of the skills will be used in the solutions of a problem, provided that the child does possess these skills. Children do not spontaneously develop the skills; they must be given the opportunities to acquire them.

As stated earlier, we believe that most teachers have not learned through inquiry; therefore, they may not be familiar with, or be able to use, the various skills that are a part of the inquiry process. We have identified some of the skills of inquiry and utilized them in the investigations in this book. It is our hope that as you become involved in these investigations, you will acquire a better understanding of these skills and will be better able to encourage the inquiry process in your classroom. The inquiry skills used in the investigations are:

1. *Observation:*   The ability to:
   (a)   Collect data through the use of the five senses.
   (b)   Construct statements of observations in qualitative and quantitative terms.
2. *Comparison:*   The ability to recognize and state similarities and differences among objects, events, and places.
3. *Identification:*   The ability to:
   (a)   Name objects, events, and places.
   (b)   Select from several alternates the designated object, event, place, or sequence.
   (c)   Devise a method to measure the properties of objects.
4. *Classification:*   The ability to:
   (a)   Form groups based on one or more common observed properties.
   (b)   Construct a graph from a table of data.
5. *Measurement:*   The ability to quantify an observation using a frame of reference.
6. *Inference:*   The ability to:
   (a)   Construct a nonobservable judgment from a set of observations and comparisons.
   (b)   Interpret a table of data.
7. *Prediction:*   The ability to state a future occurrence based on previous observations.
8. *Verification:*   The ability to check or test the accuracy of a prediction.
9. *Formulation of hypotheses:*   The ability to construct an answer to a problem from generalized observations and comparisons.
10. *Isolation of variables:*   The ability to:
   (a)   Discriminate among factors that will, and will not, affect the outcome of an experiment.
   (b)   Identify those factors which are held constant and those factors which are manipulated.
11. *Experimentation:*   The ability to:
   (a)   Recognize and formulate a problem.
   (b)   Plan and conduct a test of an hypothesis.
   (c)   Use the collected results and pose possible answers to the problem.

Curricula for Inquiry Teaching   During recent years, there have been extensive efforts to develop curricula that would help teachers to utilize inquiry in their classrooms. Committees composed of educators, psychologists, and scientists were established in order to develop curricula to accomplish this task. Each of these curricula has certain characteristics in common, for example: (1) development of inquiry skills; (2) active student participation in the learning process; and (3) the inclusion of only a few major science principles, which are studied in considerable depth. The ultimate goal of these curricula is *the development of independent learners equipped with the content, skills, and attitudes required for an ever-changing environment.*

With the publication of these curricula, there has been a tendency to utilize conceptual schemes rather than the traditional content areas. Conceptual schemes help children to see science as an interrelated field, rather than as separate fields of study, such as biology, chemistry, astronomy, and so on.

The emphasis in these curricula is on activities. As the child participates, he is provided with first-hand experiences in using the skills of inquiry. The teacher no longer demonstrates or tells the children that a white powder contains starch if it turns bluish-black when mixed with iodine. Instead, children are given a number of white powders in order to find ways of identifying them. Children taste, smell, feel, and observe rather than memorize what the teacher says and does. These curricula involve the children in many first-hand experiences. During the elementary school years, children need the opportunity to try things, to handle objects, and to manipulate materials.

The child no longer hears about *the* "scientific method," but he does hear such words as observation, collection of data, formulation of hypotheses, verification, prediction, and the making inferences. Where the emphasis in the older curricula was on accumulating content, the emphasis in the new curricula is on using skills to answer a variety of questions.

As you perform the investigations in this book, you will be investigating problems that are similar to the problems being investigated by children using these newer curricula. Therefore, these investigations should help you to feel more comfortable teaching in a school that uses these curricula. These investigations should also help you to write lessons encouraging children to inquire, even though your school has not adopted a newer curriculum.

Using This Book   Many teachers are not yet teaching science through inquiry. The new curricular programs are a good beginning; a didactic teacher, however, will teach these programs didactically. We have observed that many teachers who attempt to implement these new science curricula use the traditional "teaching-by-telling method," thus failing to alter their teaching techniques to accommodate the purposes of these programs. As a consequence, these teaching techniques may limit the extent to which the newer science curricula achieve their intended purposes.

We believe that these didactic teachers really want to teach science so that the children develop content, inquiry skills, attitudes, appreciations, and interests. They do not know, however, how to encourage this type of learning, because they have not had opportunities to learn through inquiry. We hope that the investigations in this book will help such teachers acquire the content, skills, attitudes, appreciations, and interests needed in order to teach science through inquiry. This can be achieved only if these teachers actually get involved with manipulating materials, collecting and mentally processing data.

We hope that those of you who have never taught will never be didactic teachers. After completing many of the investigations in this book, you should develop an understanding of the skills of inquiry, along with some of the principles of science, which in turn should help you to feel relatively comfortable teaching science to children.

Because the investigations are skill-centered, "open-ended," and arranged around conceptual schemes, they are of use to people with varying backgrounds. Each of you will, therefore, approach the investigations differently, depending upon this background. Those with a strong background in science might make involved hypotheses and execute very complex experiments requiring the control of several variables, while others might concentrate primarily on making observations and comparisons. Both groups are actually working together to add to the data obtained by the group as a whole. With this approach, each of you is a fully contributing member of the class.

You may begin with any investigation in this book. Some are dependent upon others, but the majority are independent of each other. In each investigation you will practice some inquiry skills and become acquainted with one aspect of a conceptual scheme. Since the skills that we have identified are a necessary part of the inquiry process, it is important for you to practice them prior to working with school-age children. The investigations will also aid you in exploring a few of the many principles of science within a conceptual scheme.

For each investigation the materials and the quantities necessary to complete them are given. If there are thirty students in your class, and each is going to do the investigation, the quantity of materials will have to be multiplied by thirty. If six of you are to work together, there would then be five groups of six students each, the quantity of each material must then be multiplied by five.

Appendix Six identifies all the objectives that are a part of each conceptual scheme. Therefore, all the objectives for all the investigations for Conceptual Scheme I are found together, then all the objectives for Conceptual Scheme II are grouped together, and so on. Appendix Seven groups the objectives according to the inquiry skill emphasized in the objective. All of the objectives attempting to increase the skill of observation are grouped together in this appendix, all of those objectives emphasizing the skill of comparison are then grouped together, and so on. There is also an outline of the science content included in Appendix Eight. This outline may help you determine how strong or weak you are in science content.

We hope that you enjoy doing some of the investigations in this book. We also hope that this book and its companion book, *Teaching Elementary School Science: Why and How,* will help you to be an outstanding teacher of elementary school science.

KENNETH D. GEORGE
MAUREEN A. DIETZ
EUGENE C. ABRAHAM

Science Investigations for
Elementary School Teachers

Matter and Energy Interact Between Living CONCEPTUAL
Organisms and Their Environment SCHEME

I

Investigation One

I. Objectives of this investigation

The student should be able to:

A. Grow plants in red, green, and blue light, sunlight, and darkness.

B. Compare the characteristics of plants grown in red, green, and blue light, sunlight, and darkness.

C. Formulate hypotheses regarding the differences in the characteristics of plants grown in red, green, and blue light, sunlight, and darkness.

D. Isolate the variables that affect the characteristics of plants grown in red, green, and blue light, sunlight, and darkness.

E. Plan and conduct an experiment to explain the differences in the characteristics of plants grown in red, green, and blue light, sunlight, and darkness.

F. Make predictions regarding the characteristics of plants grown in red-green, red-blue, and blue-green light.

G. Verify the predictions regarding the characteristics of plants grown in red-green, red-blue, and blue-green light.

H. Infer an explanation for the characteristics of trees growing in a dense forest.

II. Materials

A. Five shoe boxes

B. Single-edged razor blade

C. Cellophane tape

D. Cellophane: red, green, blue, and transparent, enough to cover shoe box lid

E. Five paper cups (with holes in the bottom made with darning needles) on small containers to catch water

F. Vermiculite or soil to fill at least 5 paper cups

G. Fifty seeds (mung, pea, corn, or wheat)

H. Five rubber bands

I. Water

1

III. Procedure

A. How do the characteristics of plants grown in red, green, and blue light, sunlight, and in darkness compare?

1. Using a single-edged razor blade, cut out most of the centers of four of the five lids from the shoe boxes (Figure 1-1).

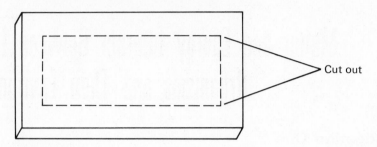

Cut out

FIGURE 1-1
Shoe Box Lid

2. Tape red cellophane over the cut-out portion of one shoe box lid. Repeat this procedure with each of the three other lids, using the green, blue, and transparent cellophane.

3. Put vermiculite or soil in five paper cups and plant seeds in each cup. Put the same amount of seeds in each cup (there should be at least ten seeds in each cup). Water the plants, using the same amount for each cup. Why is it important to keep the number of seeds and amount of water the same? Place the cups on small containers so that the excess water will drain through the holes in the cup and be caught.

4. Put one cup in each of the five shoe boxes (see Figure 1-2), and re-place the lids. Use rubber bands to hold the lids on the boxes. Place all the shoe boxes on a windowsill, with the lids facing toward the window. Four cups will then be exposed to red, green, and blue light, and sunlight and one cup will be in darkness.

5. Add the same amount of water to each cup about three times a week, being careful not to over-water.

6. Two weeks after the seeds germinate, remove the cups from the boxes. Observe and list any differences in the characteristics of the plants. How do the plants compare?

B. How can you explain the differences in the characteristics of plants grown in red, green, and blue light, sunlight, and darkness? Your answers to this question are hypotheses. Hypotheses are tested by doing an experiment.

1. What are the variables that must be controlled in order to test your hypotheses?

2. Plan and conduct an experiment to explain the differences in the characteristics of plants grown in red, green, and blue light, sunlight, and darkness (this is the test for your hypotheses).

FIGURE 1-2
Cup in Shoe Box

C. What predictions can you make regarding the characteristics of plants grown in red-green, red-blue, and blue-green light?
   1. Predict the characteristics of plants grown in red-green, red-blue, and blue-green light.
   2. Verify your predictions by growing plants in boxes that have openings covered with the following combinations of colored cellophane: red-green, red-blue, and blue-green.
D. What are the characteristics of trees growing in a dense forest? Based on data collected in this investigation, infer an explanation for these characteristics.

Investigation Two

I. Objectives of this investigation

The student should be able to:

A. Identify the direction that plants grow in relation to a light source.

B. Infer an explanation for the direction that plants grow in relation to a light source.

C. Compare the heights of plants grown under varying proportions of light and dark.

D. Graph the height of a plant against the number of hours of light per 24 hours that the plant received.

E. Infer an explanation for the different heights of plants grown under varying proportions of light and dark.

F. Infer a relationship between the direction plants grow and the proportion of light they receive.

II. Materials

A. One plant

B. Vermiculite or soil (to fill paper cup)

C. At least 6 paper cups (with holes in the bottom—made with darning needles) on small containers to catch water

D. At least 60 seeds (mung, pea, or corn)

E. Water

F. Metric ruler

III. Procedure

A. Place a plant near a window and observe it for several days (without moving the plant). In what direction is the plant growing in relation to the window? What inference can you make to explain your observation?

B. How do varying proportions of light and dark affect the growth of plants?

1. Put vermiculite or soil in at least six paper cups, and plant at least ten seeds in each cup. Put the same amount of water in each cup. Place the cups on small containers so that the excess water that drains through the holes in the cup will be caught.

2. Place all your cups in the same location until the seeds germinate and the plants have their first leaves. Measure (in centimeters) the height of the plants in each cup. Average the height of the plants in each cup and record this information.

3. Up to this point, your plants have had similar proportions of light and dark during each 24-hour period. What effect would different proportions of light and dark have on the continued growth of these plants? In order to answer this question, plants would have to be placed in varying proportions of light and dark. One cup and its plants should receive 24 hours of light and no darkness. Another cup and its plants should be in constant darkness. Between these two extremes, plants should be placed in varying proportions of light and dark, for example, 3 hours of light and 21 hours of dark, 6 hours of

4

light and 18 hours of dark, and so on. The plants should be grown under these conditions for two weeks. Remember to control all the variables, except for the proportions of light and dark that the plants receive.

4. About three times a week, add the same amount of water to each cup, being careful not to over-water.

5. After two weeks, measure (in centimeters) the height of the plants in each cup. Average the height of the plants in each cup and record this information. Which plants grew the most and which plants grew the least? Graph the *average gain* in height of the plants against the number of hours of light per 24 hours that the plant received, using the graph in Figure 1-3 as a guide.

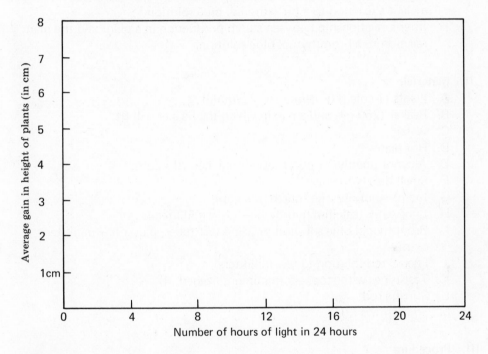

FIGURE 1-3
Graph of Average Height of Plants vs. Number of Hours of Light per 24 Hours

6. How would you interpret the graph concerning the effect of varying proportions of light and dark on the growth of plants? What inferences can you make to explain this effect? How do these inferences compare with the inferences you made regarding the characteristics of plants grown in red, green, and blue light, sunlight, and darkness in Investigation One?

C. Infer a relationship between the direction plants grow and the proportion of light they receive. What explanation can you now give for the direction a plant grows in relation to a source of light, such as the sun?

Investigation Three

I. **Objectives of this investigation**
  The student should be able to:
  A. Verify the presence of starch in the leaves of plants.
  B. Isolate the variables that will affect the production of starch in plants.
  C. Plan and conduct an experiment to determine those variables that will affect the production of starch in plants.
  D. Verify the presence of carbon dioxide in your breath.
  E. Formulate an hypothesis to explain why a bromthymol blue solution changes color when a plant is placed in the solution.
  F. Isolate the variables that will affect a plant's reaction to a bromthymol blue solution.
  G. Plan and conduct an experiment to determine which variables will affect a plant's reaction to a bromthymol blue solution.
  H. Infer a relationship between starch production in a plant and the plant's reaction to a bromthymol blue solution.

II. **Materials**
  A. Plants (1 coleus or geranium, 2 *Elodea*)
  B. Beaker (250 ml) and a pan in which the beaker will fit
  C. Water
  D. Hot plate
  E. Alcohol (methyl or ethyl—about one-half of a cup)
  F. Small dish with cover
  G. Iodine solution (one-fourth of a cup)
  H. Limewater (calcium hydroxide—a few milliliters)
  I. Bromthymol blue solution (to fill 4 test tubes, plus a few milliliters extra)
  J. Phenol red solution (a few milliliters)
  K. Test tubes with stoppers (minimum needed: 4)
  L. Stirring rod
  M. Soda straws (2)

III. **Procedure**
  A. The following activity can be done to verify the presence of starch in the leaves of a plant.
    1. Remove a leaf from a coleus or a geranium plant and put it in a beaker of water. Place the beaker of water, with the leaf, on an electric hot plate and boil for a few minutes. Pour off the water and pour in enough alcohol to cover the leaf. The alcohol will remove the chlorophyll from the leaf. Place the beaker in a pan of water and place the pan on the hot plate. Boil the water for about ten minutes. Stir the alcohol and the leaf. **Danger: never heat alcohol over an open flame, as it easily ignites.**
    2. Remove the leaf from the alcohol and rinse with water. Place the leaf in a small dish and cover it for about five minutes with a dilute solution of iodine. Rinse the leaf with water.

6

3. Hold the leaf up to a light. Observe the blackish parts of the leaf. When iodine is added to starch, the starch turns blue-black.

B. What variables might influence the production of starch in leaves of plants? In Investigation Two you observed the effects of various proportions of light and dark on the height of the plant. Do these variables affect the production of starch in a geranium or a coleus plant?

1. Plan and conduct an experiment to determine those variables which will affect the production of starch in plants.

2. Control all the variables in the experiment except for the one being studied.

C. The following activity can be done to verify the presence of carbon dioxide.

1. When you exhale, carbon dioxide is present in your breath.

2. Limewater (calcium hydroxide), bromthymol blue solution, or phenol red solution are used to indicate the presence of carbon dioxide.

3. Blow through a soda straw into a few milliliters of limewater in a test tube. Repeat, blowing into a few milliliters of a bromthymol blue solution in another test tube and then into another test tube containing a few milliliters of a phenol red solution.

4. Record what happens to each of the solutions when you blow into them and then clean the test tubes. These solutions are used to indicate the presence of carbon dioxide.

D. How does a plant affect a bromthymol blue solution?

1. Fill four test tubes almost to the top with a bromthymol blue solution. Blow through a soda straw into two of the four test tubes so that the presence of carbon dioxide is indicated. Place a small *Elodea* plant in one of the test tubes that you blew into and another *Elodea* plant in one of the test tubes that you did not blow into. Put a stopper in each of the four test tubes. Place the tubes in the sunlight. Observe the test tubes for two days.

2. What do you observe in the four test tubes? Why did you need two test tubes without plants for this investigation?

3. Formulate an hypothesis to explain your observations.

4. What variables will affect a reaction between a plant and bromthymol blue solution? Plan and conduct an experiment to determine which of the variables you identified will affect a plant's reaction to a bromthymol blue solution. Prepare as many test tubes as you will need with a bromthymol blue solution and an *Elodea* plant. Remember to keep one test tube without a plant (but everything else should be the same in all the test tubes). All variables must be the same, except for the variable you are investigating.

E. What relationship exists between starch production in a plant and the plant's reaction to a bromthymol blue solution? Which variables studied in this investigation help you to answer this question?

Investigation Four

I. Objectives of this investigation

The student should be able to:

A. Compare a system containing a phenol red solution and a plant with a system containing a phenol red solution and an animal, both systems having been kept in the light for 24 hours.

B. Infer an explanation for the similarities and differences in two systems (plant and phenol red solution; animal and phenol red solution) that have been kept in the light for 24 hours.

C. Make predictions regarding the effect of plants and animals on phenol red solutions after the systems have been in the dark for 24 hours.

D. Verify the predictions regarding the effect of plants and animals on phenol red solutions after the systems have been in the dark for 24 hours.

E. Compare the effects of plants and animals on phenol red solutions placed in the light for 24 hours and in the dark for 24 hours.

F. Infer an explanation for the comparison of phenol red solutions placed in the light for 24 hours and in the dark for 24 hours, one system containing plants and the other system containing animals.

II. Materials

A. Eight test tubes with a stopper for each tube
B. Phenol red solution (about 40 drops)
C. Medicine dropper
D. Brads (8 to 16)
E. *Elodea* plant (2)
F. Twenty to thirty germinating seeds
G. Living insect (2)
H. Source of light
I. Test tube rack (2)

III. Procedure

A. Review Investigation Three on the effect of (1) carbon dioxide on a phenol red solution and (2) of a plant on a bromthymol blue solution.

B. How will a plant affect a phenol red solution? How will an animal affect a phenol red solution?

1. Number four test tubes.

2. Put a few drops of a phenol red solution into each of the four test tubes. Place enough brads into each of the four test tubes so that the plants and animals placed in the tubes are prevented from coming in direct contact with the phenol red solution.

3. (a) Stopper tube 1.
   (b) Place ten to fifteen germinating seeds in tube 2 and stopper it.
   (c) Place a living insect (fly, beetle, or such) in tube 3 and stopper it.
   (d) Place a piece of an *Elodea* plant in tube 4 and stopper it.
   (e) Each of the four tubes and its contents is called a *system.*

4. Place the four systems in a test tube rack and place this under a

source of light for 24 hours. Observe the systems and record your observations. What has happened to the phenol red solution in each of the systems? Which systems are similar in appearance? How are they similar? Which systems are different in appearance? How are they different?

5. Infer an explanation for your observations of the four systems kept in the light for 24 hours.

C. What effect will a plant and an animal have on a phenol red solution when the system is kept in the dark for 24 hours?

1. Predict the effect a plant and an animal will have on a phenol red solution when the system is kept in the dark for 24 hours.

2. Repeat steps B-1 to B-3, and then place the four systems in a completely dark location for 24 hours.

3. How accurate was your prediction?

4. Compare the systems placed in the dark for 24 hours with the systems placed in the light for 24 hours.

5. Infer an explanation for the comparisons of the systems that have been in the light for 24 hours and the systems that have been in the dark for 24 hours.

Investigation Five

I. Objectives of this investigation

The student should be able to:

A. Compare lima beans, raisins, and prunes soaked in water with those not soaked in water.

B. Make inferences to explain the differences among soaked and unsoaked lima beans, raisins, and prunes.

C. Compare the changes that take place in and around three pieces of dialysis tubing soaked in water: one piece containing sugar and water, one piece containing corn syrup, and the third piece containing water.

D. Formulate an hypothesis to explain the changes that occur in and around three pieces of dialysis tubing soaked in water: one piece containing sugar and water; one piece containing corn syrup; and the third piece containing water.

E. Plan and conduct an experiment to explain the changes that occur in and around three pieces of dialysis tubing soaked in water: one piece containing sugar and water; one piece containing corn syrup; and the third piece containing water.

F. Predict the similarities of plastic wrap, wax paper, and cellophane with dialysis tubing.

G. Verify the predictions of the similarities of plastic wrap, wax paper, and cellophane with dialysis tubing.

H. Infer an explanation for the passage of water into a plant.

II. Materials

A. Three glass jars with lids

B. Graduated cylinder

C. Metric ruler

D. Water

E. Dried prunes (with the seeds), raisins, and lima beans (4 of each)

F. Three pieces of dialysis tubing or sausage casing (25 cm long by 5 cm wide)

G. Scissors

H. Sugar (40 ml)

I. Corn syrup (45 ml)

J. Plastic wrap, wax paper, cellophane (enough to form a small bag)

III. Procedure

A. Place four dried prunes, four raisins, and four lima beans in separate glass jars. Fill these three jars about two-thirds full of water, measuring and recording the amount of water in milliliters. Place the lids tightly on the jars and let them stand for 24 hours. Examine the prunes, raisins, and lima beans. How do they compare with unsoaked prunes, raisins, and lima beans? How does the amount of water compare with the amount originally placed in the jar?

B. What inferences can you make to explain the differences among soaked and unsoaked prunes, raisins, and lima beans?

10

C. What properties would a prune, raisin, and lima bean have in common with each other in order to make your inference correct?

    1. Soak the three pieces of dialysis tubing or sausage casing in water for a few minutes to soften them.

    2. Tie a knot in one end of each of the three pieces and blow into the other end to open the tube or casing.

    3. Each of the three tubes can then be filled with the following:

        Tube *A*: 20 ml of sugar and 5 ml of water
        Tube *B*: 25 ml of corn syrup
        Tube *C*: 25 ml of water

    4. Squeeze the air out of the tubes and knot the other end.

    5. Put each of the three tubes into separate glass jars which are about two-thirds full of water. (Measure and record the amount of water in milliliters.) Place the lids tightly on the jars.

    6. Observe the systems (the tube and surrounding liquid) during the next 24-hour period.

    7. How do the three systems compare with each other? How have the systems changed since the beginning of the investigation? Use measurements whenever possible in order to make your comparisons more accurate.

    8. Formulate an hypothesis to explain the changes that occur in the three systems.

    9. Plan and conduct an experiment to test your hypothesis.

    10. Based on this experiment, what inferences can you make to explain the differences in soaked and unsoaked prunes, raisins, and lima beans?

D. Will systems containing plastic wrap, wax paper, or cellophane change in the same manner as the dialysis tubing systems changed?

    1. Verify your prediction by repeating the process you used in part C, only forming small bags with plastic wrap, wax paper, or cellophane.

    2. What inferences can you make about these three materials?

    3. How do these inferences compare with the inferences you made regarding the dialysis tubing and the properties of the prune, raisin, and lima beans?

E. Based on data collected in this investigation, infer an explanation for the passage of water into a plant.

Investigation Six

I. **Objectives of this investigation**
   The student should be able to:
   A. Observe and list the characteristics of mealworms.
   B. Formulate hypotheses concerning the abilities of the mealworms to see, hear, and smell.
   C. Plan and conduct experiments to test the hypotheses concerning the ability of the mealworms to see, hear, and smell.
   D. Formulate hypotheses concerning the foods that the mealworms prefer to eat.
   E. Plan and conduct experiments to test the hypotheses concerning the foods that the mealworms prefer to eat.

II. **Materials**
   A. Mealworms (5 to 10)
   B. Paper plate
   C. Small hand lens
   D. Assorted foods, such as cereal, vegetables, and fruit

III. **Procedure**
   A. What are the characteristics of mealworms?
      1. Place several mealworms on a paper plate and observe them for several minutes.
      2. How do you know that they are alive? How could you verify that they are actually living?
      3. How are the mealworms alike and how are they different? List these similarities and differences.
      4. What additional observations can you make with the aid of the small hand lens? Record these additional observations.
   B. Based on your observations of the mealworms, formulate hypotheses concerning their ability to see, hear, and smell.
      1. Plan and conduct experiments to test your hypotheses.
      2. What variables must be controlled in each experiment? Are there any variables which cannot be controlled?
   C. What types of foods do the mealworms prefer?
      1. From your observations of the mealworms, what hypotheses can you make concerning the foods that the mealworms prefer to eat?
      2. Plan and conduct experiments in order to test the hypotheses concerning the kinds of foods that the mealworms prefer to eat.

Investigation Seven

I. Objectives of this investigation
The student should be able to:
A. Set up an aquarium.
B. Observe and list the changes that occur in an aquarium over an extended period of time.
C. Formulate an hypothesis to explain the changes that occur in an aquarium.
D. Isolate the variables involved in tests regarding changes in an aquarium.
E. Plan and conduct an experiment to investigate the causes of changes in an aquarium.
F. Infer a relationship of plants and animals in an aquarium.

II. Materials
A. Gallon jar
B. Water
C. Sand (to cover bottom of jar to a depth of 2 cm)
D. Water plants, such as *Elodea* and duckweed
E. Water snails (at least 3)
F. Guppies (2 males and 2 females)

III. Procedure
A. What changes occur in an aquarium over an extended period of time?
   1. Place an aquarium near a window where it will receive light. (See Appendix 1-1: Techniques for Establishing an Aquarium.)
   2. Observe and keep a daily list of all the changes that occur in the aquarium. What variables might have caused these changes to occur?
B. Plan and conduct an experiment to determine which variables caused changes in the aquarium.
   1. Construct hypotheses to explain the observed changes in the aquarium.
   2. Isolate the variables that might have caused these changes.
   3. Plan and conduct an experiment to test each hypothesis.
C. What inferences can you make regarding the relationship of plants and animals in an aquarium?

CONCEPTUAL SCHEME II Matter Can Be Measured in Mathematical Units and These Units Exist in Orderly Systems

Investigation One

I. Objectives of this investigation

The students should be able to:

A. Measure the distance between markings in this book, in metric units.

B. Measure the volume of a solid and of a liquid, in metric units.

C. Compare the change in the volume of water in a container with the volume of a solid object when it is submerged in the water.

D. Identify a procedure to measure, in metric units, the volume of an irregular shaped object.

II. Materials

A. Metric ruler

B. Measuring cup

C. Graduated cylinder

D. Medicine dropper

E. Rectangular block of metal (small enough to fit inside the graduated cylinder)

F. Small stone

G. Meterstick

III. Procedure

A. In metric units, how far apart are the markings in this book? How accurately can the distance between two points be measured?

1. Place a metric ruler in the position indicated in Figure 2-1. (See Appendix 2-1: Reading a Meterstick.)

2. Measure the distance from point *A* to point *B* and from point *B* to point *C*. Record these measurements. If the markings on the metric ruler do not fall directly under points *A*, *B*, or *C*, estimate the distances. (See Appendix 2-2: Estimating Distances.)

B. How is the change in the volume of water in the container related to the volume of a solid object submerged in that water?

1. (See Appendix 2-3: Measuring Liquid Volume.) Fill a measuring cup half full of water. Pour the water into the graduated cylinder until it

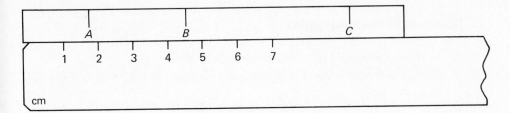

FIGURE 2-1
Metric Ruler and Distances to Measure

reaches the 15-ml mark. If the water is not quite at the 15-ml mark, use a medicine dropper to add or remove water until there is exactly 15 ml of water in the cylinder.

2. Using your metric ruler, measure the length, width, and height (in centimeters) of a rectangular block of metal. Using metric units, calculate the volume (length X width X height) of the metal. Record this information.

3. Take the rectangular block of metal and slowly lower the block into the graduated cylinder containing the 15 ml of water. What do you observe after the rectangular block has been lowered to the bottom of the cylinder?

4. How does the volume of the rectangular block found in step 2 compare with the change in the water volume observed in step 3?

C. Identify a procedure to measure, in metric units, the volume of an irregular shaped object, such as a small stone.

Investigation Two

I. Objectives of this investigation

The students should be able to:

A. Measure the weight of an object in metric units.

B. Predict the weight of a metal block in air, cooking oil, vinegar, and motor oil.

C. Verify the predictions concerning the weight of a metal block in air, cooking oil, vinegar, and motor oil.

D. Compare the weight in water of a metal, wooden, plastic, and aluminum foil block.

E. Isolate the variables which affect the weight of different blocks of materials placed in several different liquids.

F. Plan and conduct an experiment to determine which variables affect the weight of different blocks of materials placed in several different liquids.

G. Predict the results of placing a sheet of aluminum foil and a ball of foil on the surface of a liquid.

H. Verify the predictions concerning the results of placing a sheet of aluminum foil and a ball of aluminum foil on the surface of a liquid.

I. Infer an explanation as to why boats float.

II. Materials

A. Water, cooking oil, vinegar, motor oil (¾ cup of each)

B. Spring balance

C. Strong thread (50 cm)

D. Metal, wood, plastic, and aluminum foil blocks (the same size and small enough to fit inside a measuring cup)

E. Measuring cup

F. A 4-in. square of aluminum foil

G. A bowl (cereal type)

III. Procedure

A. What is the relationship between the weight of an object in air and in various liquids?

1. Tie a strong thread around the metal block and loop the other end of the thread around the hook of the spring balance. (See Figure 2-2.) Weigh and record the weight of the block.

2. Predict the weight of the metal block when it is suspended in water, cooking oil, vinegar, and motor oil. Verify your predictions by filling the measuring cup with one liquid at a time and lower the metal block (still hooked to the spring balance) into the liquid. (See Figure 2-2.) Read the scale before and after the block is submerged in each liquid and record this information in the table in Figure 2-3.

3. Repeat the procedure of steps 2 and 3, using the blocks made of different materials. Complete the table in Figure 2-3.

4. Compare the weight in water of the metal block with the weight in water of the wooden, plastic, and aluminum foil blocks.

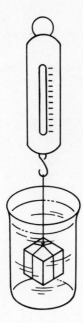 

FIGURE 2-2
Block Suspended from a Spring Balance In and Out of a Liquid

Object (block of)	Wgt. in air	Wgt. in water	Wgt. in oil (cooking)	Wgt. in vinegar	Wgt. in motor oil
Metal					
Wood					
Plastic					
Aluminum foil					

FIGURE 2-3
Table for Comparison of the Weight of an Object in Air and in Liquids

5. Isolate the variables which affect the weight of different material blocks placed in several different liquids.
6. Plan and conduct an experiment to determine which variables affect the weight of different blocks of materials placed in several different liquids.

B. Why does a boat float? Can an object both float and sink in the same liquid?
1. Fill the soup or cereal bowl with water.
2. Predict what will happen when you place the 4-in. square of aluminum foil on the surface of the water in the bowl. Verify your prediction.
3. Remove the sheet of foil from the water and roll the sheet into a ball. Predict what will happen when you place the ball of aluminum foil on the water. Verify your prediction.

III. **Procedure** *(continued)*

4. Repeat steps 1 to 3 using the cooking oil, the vinegar, and the motor oil. Record all your observations.
5. Based on these observations, predictions, and comparisons, infer why a boat floats.

Investigation Three

I. Objectives of this investigation
The students should be able to:
  A. Compare the weight of equal volumes of water, alcohol, olive oil, pentane, and turpentine.
  B. Infer why all liquids do or do not have the same weight.
  C. Compare the weight/volume ratio of water with the weight/volume ratio of alcohol, olive oil, pentane, and turpentine.
  D. Predict whether ice will float on alcohol, olive oil, pentane, and turpentine.
  E. Verify the predictions concerning whether ice will float on alcohol, olive oil, pentane, and turpentine.

II. Materials
  A. Pan balance (scale)
  B. Graduated cylinders (10 ml, 50 ml, 100 ml)
  C. Measuring cup
  D. Water, alcohol, olive oil, pentane, turpentine (200 ml of each)
  E. Five ice cubes of approximately the same size

III. Procedure
  A. Do all liquids have the same weight?
    1. See Investigation One for the relationship between volume measured in cubic centimeters and volume measured in milliliters.
    2. Using a pan balance or scale, weigh and record (in grams) the 10-ml graduated cylinder. Pour exactly 10 ml of water from the measuring cup into the cylinder. Weigh and record the weight of the cylinder plus the water. What is the weight of the water alone? What would be the weight of one milliliter of water?
    3. Repeat step 2 with various volumes of water and complete the table in Figure 2-4.
    4. Repeat steps 2 and 3 weighing 1, 10, 50, and 100 ml of alcohol, olive oil, pentane, and turpentine. Construct a table similar to Figure 2-4 in order to record your data.
    5. Compare the weights of the other liquids with the weight of water. Infer a reason why all liquids do or do not have the same weight.

Volume of water (ml)	Weight of water (grams)
1 Milliliter	
10 Milliliters	
50 Milliliters	
100 Milliliters	

FIGURE 2-4
Table for Weight Related to Volume

III. **Procedure** *(continued)*

B. Will ice float on all liquids?

1. Re-read Investigation Two to identify the factors that determine whether an object floats.
2. Based on Investigation Two and the comparisons made above, predict whether an ice cube will float on water, olive oil, pentane, and turpentine.
3. Verify your predictions.

Investigation Four

I. Objectives of this investigation

The students should be able to:

A. Measure temperature, in both Fahrenheit and Celsius units.

B. Hypothesize reasons for the different temperature readings recorded throughout the classroom.

C. Predict the temperature, in both Fahrenheit and Celsius units, of various locations outside the classroom.

D. Verify the predictions concerning the temperature of various locations outside the classroom.

II. Materials

A. Thermometer, with Fahrenheit and Celsius units

B. Ice cubes (6 to 8)

C. Water (enough to fill half the Pyrex beaker)

D. Heat source (for example, hot plate)

E. Pyrex beaker

III. Procedure

A. What are the similarities and differences between the Fahrenheit (F) and Celsius (C) temperature scales?

1. In Investigation One you determined the height of liquid in a graduated cylinder. Using that same procedure, read your thermometer and record the temperature of your location in the classroom in both Fahrenheit and Celsius units. These units are found on the two scales printed on the thermometer.

2. Compare the temperatures recorded by the different members of your class. If these recordings are not the same, hypothesize reason(s) for the differences.

3. Place your thermometer in a beaker of water and ice cubes. Record the temperature of the ice-water mixture. Stir the mixture gently with the thermometer, recording both the Fahrenheit and Celsius readings every two or three minutes. What do you observe about the temperature readings? What is the temperature reading before the ice is melted? After the ice has melted?

4. Place the Pyrex beaker with the melted ice over a source of heat, such as a hot plate. Bring the water to a boil, while gently stirring the water with the thermometer, being careful not to let the thermometer touch the Pyrex beaker. Record both Fahrenheit and Celsius readings every two or three minutes during heating. What do you observe about the temperature readings? What is the temperature of the water before boiling? During boiling?

5. Estimate the temperature of the air in the beaker after all the water has boiled away.

6. From the data collected in steps 3 and 4, designate one thermometer reading as the "bottom" reading and one as the "top" reading. Do this for both the Fahrenheit and Celsius scales.

III. Procedure *(continued)*

7. How many degrees are there between the "top" and "bottom" readings on the Fahrenheit and Celsius scales? List the occasions when it would be better to use the Celsius scale and those occasions when it would be better to use the Fahrenheit scale. Indicate your reasons.

B. Predict the temperature, on both the Fahrenheit and Celsius scales, of various places outside the classroom; for example, the corridor, the stairways, and the water from the drinking fountain. Verify your predictions.

Investigation Five

I. Objectives of this investigation

The students should be able to:

A. Measure the size of an angle, a circle, and a sphere, using a protractor.

B. Rank four angles in order from largest to smallest.

C. Identify the dimensions of a sphere that must be changed in order to alter the size of the whole sphere.

II. Materials

A. Protractor

B. Small ball

C. Large ball

D. String (Several feet)

E. Metric ruler

III. Procedure

A. What factors determine the size of an angle?

1. Use the protractor to measure the number of degrees in angles *A* and *B* in Figure 2-5. (See Appendix 2-4: Use of a Protractor.) Record these measurements.

2. Measure and record the number of degrees in angles *C* and *D* in Figure 2-6.

3. What is the largest angle, in degrees, that can be drawn?

B. How many degrees are there in half a circle? In a full circle?

1. Measure angle *AOB* in Figure 2-7. Record the number of degrees in this angle. An arc is a portion of a curved line, such as a circle. In

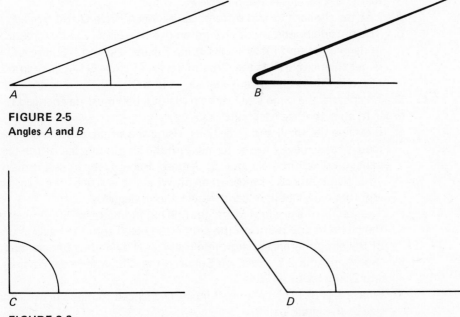

FIGURE 2-5
Angles *A* and *B*

FIGURE 2-6
Angles *C* and *D*

23

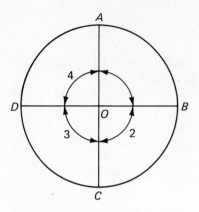

FIGURE 2-7
Circle *O*

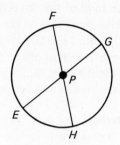

FIGURE 2-8
Circle *P*

III. Procedure *(continued)*

Figure 2-7 the section of circle *O* between *A* and *B* is an arc. Look at the size of angle *AOB* just recorded. Arc *AB* is also this size, in degrees.

2. Measure angles 2, 3, and 4 in Figure 2-7. Record each measurement and determine the size of arcs *BC, CD,* and *DA.*

3. From the data collected in steps 1 and 2, determine how many degrees there are in circle *O.*

4. In Figure 2-8, measure the number of degrees between points *E* and *F;* between points *F* and *G; G* and *H;* and *H* to *E.* How many degrees are there in circle *P?*

5. List the similarities and differences between circle *O* and circle *P.*

6. The outside boundary or circumference of a circle can be measured in degrees or centimeters. Observing Figures 2-7 and 2-8, circle *O* is larger than circle *P.* Is the circumference of circle *O* larger than that of circle *P* in degrees, centimeters, or both?

C. Are all spheres the same size? What parts of a ball must be changed in order to alter the size of a ball?

1. Examine the small and large balls. Using the string, protractor, and metric ruler, devise a way to measure the circumference of the two balls in (a) centimeters and (b) degrees. Record a brief description of your two methods of measurement. What is the size of the larger ball and the smaller ball, in centimeters and in degrees?

2. The radius of a circle is a straight line extending from the center of the circle to any point on the circumference. From the measurement of the circumference, determine the size of the radius of each ball. (See Appendix 2-5: Relation Between the Circumference, Radius, and Diameter of a Circle.)

3. What parts of the smaller ball must be changed to make it the same size as the larger ball?

Investigation Six

I. **Objectives of this investigation**

The students should be able to:

A. Measure time without using a clock or watch.

II. **Materials**

A. Marking pen or pencil

III. **Procedure**

A. Invent a measure of time between any two events; for example, between consecutive people passing the classroom door. *One restriction:* Do not use a watch or clock.

B. Record the method you invented for measuring time. What are the essential characteristics of your method?

C. Compare your timing method with the method invented by another student in your class. Measure time with the other student's method. Which characteristics identified in part B does his method have? If it does not have all the characteristics essential to your method, change his method so that it does.

CONCEPTUAL SCHEME III
Changes in Matter Require Energy and the Totality of Matter and Energy is Conserved

Investigation One

I. Objectives of this investigation
The student should be able to:
A. Predict the rate of a chemical reaction when:
1. Particle size is changed.
2. Concentration is changed.
3. Surface area is changed.
4. Temperature is changed.
B. Verify the predictions concerning the rate of a chemical reaction when:
1. Particle size is changed.
2. Concentration is changed.
3. Surface area is changed.
4. Temperature is changed.
C. Make inferences concerning the nature of chemical reactions.

II. Materials
A. Potassium permanganate (*coarse* powder, ¼ teaspoon)
B. Potassium permanganate (*fine* powder, ¼ teaspoon)
C. Glycerine (5 ml)
D. Iron powder (5 g), one piece of steel wool, one strip of iron
E. Solutions *A* and *B** (starch, water, sodium bisulfite, sulfuric acid, and potassium iodate)
F. Asbestos sheet
G. Medicine dropper and stirring rod
H. Two graduated cylinders (100 ml)
I. Wire test tube holder or tongs
J. Bunsen burner
K. Beaker (250 ml)

III. Procedure
A. What effect does decreasing particle size have on the time it takes for chemical reaction to begin?

*See Appendix 3-1: Procedure for Preparing Solutions *A* and *B*.

1. Verify your prediction by placing ¼ teaspoon of *coarse* potassium permanganate on an asbestos sheet. Make a small depression in the center of the mound and add one drop of glycerine. **Caution: Step back to observe this reaction.** Record the time it takes for the reaction to begin.
2. Would you predict that it would take more or less time for the reaction to begin if *fine* potassium permanganate were used. Determine this by using the *fine* potassium permanganate.
3. How do the times for the reactions to begin in steps 1 and 2 compare?
4. What inferences can you make about the nature of chemical reactions based on these observations and comparisons?

Reaction	Solution *A*	Solution *B*	Reaction time
(a)	20 ml	20 ml	
(b)	10 ml + 10 ml water	10 ml + 10 ml water	
(c)	5 ml + 15 ml water	5 ml + 15 ml water	
(d)	20 ml	20 ml which has been *refrigerated*	
(e)	20 ml	20 ml which has been *heated in boiling water*	

FIGURE 3-1
Proportions of Solutions *A* and *B*

B. What is the effect of concentration and temperature on the time it takes for a chemical reaction to begin?
1. Verify your predictions by using the amounts of solutions *A* and *B* as shown in the table in Figure 3-1. Measure solutions *A* and *B* in *separate* graduated cylinders, then quickly mix them together in a beaker while stirring, and begin timing. Complete the table in Figure 3-1.
2. How do the times for reactions (a), (b), and (c) from the table in Figure 3-1 compare?
3. What inferences can you make based on these data?
4. How do the times for reactions (d) and (e) from the table in Figure 3-1 compare with the time for reaction (a)?
5. What inferences can you make concerning the nature of chemical reactions based on these data?
C. Predict the effect of increasing surface area on the time it takes for a chemical reaction to begin.
1. Verify your prediction by comparing the burning rates of a strip of iron, a piece of steel wool, and iron powder over a Bunsen burner flame. Use care when "dusting" the iron powder into the flame.
2. How do the three reactions in step 1 compare?
3. What inferences concerning the nature of chemical reactions can you make based on the data in step 1?
4. How is this part of the investigation similar to steps A-1 and A-2? How are surface area and particle size related?

Investigation Two

I. **Objectives of this investigation**
   The student should be able to:
   A. Prepare and grow crystals of at least one of the following compounds:
      1. Potassium dichromate
      2. Cupric sulfate
      3. Nickelous sulfate
      4. Potassium sulfate
      5. Sodium chloride
      6. Potassium aluminum sulfate (alum)
      7. Potassium chromium sulfate (chrome alum)
   B. Predict the effect on the growth of a crystal by changing the rate of evaporation of the growing solution.
   C. Plan and conduct an experiment to determine the effect on the growth of a crystal by changing the rate of evaporation of the growing solution.
   D. Graph the rate of growth of the seed crystals.
   E. Predict the size of one crystal after one month's growth.
   F. Compare the properties of all the crystals produced and grown by the other members of the class.
   G. Predict which compound would produce the largest crystal at the end of a specified period of time.
   H. Predict the effects on the growth of a crystal by:
      1. Adding a second compound to the growing solution.
      2. Breaking the seed crystal.
   I. Plan and conduct an experiment to determine the effects on the growth of a crystal by:
      1. Adding a second compound to the growing solution.
      2. Breaking the seed crystal.
   J. Infer factors that might affect the growth of a crystal.

II. **Materials**
   A. 8 oz of one of the following compounds:
      1. Potassium dichromate
      2. Cupric sulfate
      3. Nickelous sulfate
      4. Potassium sulfate
      5. Sodium chloride
      6. Potassium aluminum sulfate
      7. Potassium chromium sulfate
   B. Empty baby food sized jars (9)
   C. Metric ruler
   D. Laboratory balance
   E. Graph paper
   F. Distilled water (500 ml)
   G. Beaker (500 ml)

III. **Procedure**
   A. How does the rate of growth of a crystal depend on the amount of

evaporation of the solution?

1. Begin the investigation by preparing at least nine seed crystals of one of the compounds identified in the list of materials. (See Appendix 3-2: Preparation of the Seed Crystals.)

2. Plan and conduct an experiment to determine the effect of the rate of evaporation of the growing solution on the growth of the seed crystals.

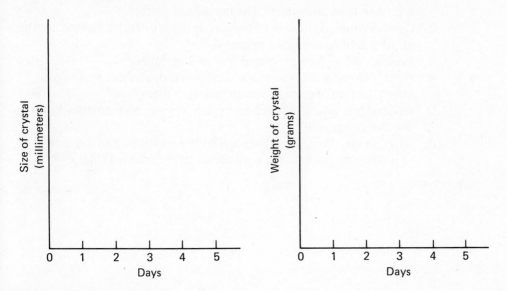

FIGURE 3-2
Graphs Showing Size and Weight of Crystals Over a Five-Day Period

3. Record the size (in millimeters) and the weight (in grams) of each of the crystals that you are growing over a five-day period. Construct graphs similar to those in Figure 3-2 for each crystal.

4. How do the sizes and weights of the crystals compare at the end of the five-day period?

5. From the graphs that you have constructed in step 3, predict the size and weight of each of the crystals after one month's growth.

6. How do the crystals that you prepared compare in appearance with those produced by other members of the class?

7. Which compound would you predict would produce the largest crystal at the end of one month? Which would produce the heaviest crystal?

B. How would the rate of growth and the appearance of a crystal be changed by the addition of a second compound to the growing solution?

1. Plan and conduct an experiment to determine the effect of a second compound in the growing solution on the growth of a crystal.

2. How do the crystals produced in step 1 compare?

3. Record the rate of growth of each of the crystals by making graphs

III. Procedure *(continued)*

as outlined in step A-3.

4. What inferences about crystal growth can you make based on your data?

C. What happens to a growing crystal when it is broken and allowed to continue growing?

1. Plan and conduct an experiment to determine the effects on crystal growth when the seed crystal is broken. Does the way that the crystal is broken have any effect? The number of pieces?

2. Carefully record the rate of growth of the crystals by making another set of graphs as described in step A-3.

3. How do the crystals produced in step 1 compare?

4. What inferences can you make concerning the factors that might affect the rate of crystal growth based on these data?

5. What results would you expect in step 1 if you used crystals from another compound?

6. What do you think would happen to the appearance of a crystal if two different compounds were added to the growing solution?

Investigation Three

I. Objectives of this investigation

The student should be able to:

A. Compare the properties of three water samples before and after:
   1. Boiling for five minutes.
   2. Filtering through filter paper.
   3. Filtering through filter paper and activated charcoal.
   4. Distillation.
B. Identify a procedure to remove the greatest number of impurities from a water sample.
C. Plan and conduct an experiment, using the identified procedure, to purify a water sample.
D. Infer the properties of water samples found:
   1. At the base of a waterfall.
   2. In a polluted river.
   3. In the ocean.
   4. In a stagnant lake.
   5. In a fast flowing mountain stream.

II. Materials

A. Water samples *A, B,* and *C* (water, soil, sodium chloride, food coloring, ammonia, and vinegar) See Appendix 3-3.
B. Filter paper and funnel
C. Five test tubes
D. Distilling apparatus (250-ml flask, tubing, stopper, collecting jar, and pneumatic trough) See Appendix 3-3 for preparation of distillation apparatus.
E. Activated charcoal (1 oz)
F. Six beakers (250 ml)
G. Bunsen burner, tripod, wire screen

III. Procedure

A. What are some methods of removing impurities from samples of water?
   1. Observe and list the physical characteristics of the three water samples (*A, B,* and *C*) and add these data to the table in Figure 3-3.
   2. Place 100 ml of each sample in separate beakers and boil for two minutes. After five minutes of cooling, again observe and list the properties in the table in Figure 3-3.

Sample	Initially	After boiling	After filtering	After filtering plus charcoal	After distillation
A					
B					
C					

FIGURE 3-3
Properties of the Water Samples

III. **Procedure** *(continued)*

      3. How do your lists of observations compare?

      4. What impurities, if any, seem to have been removed? What evidence do you have to support your conclusions?

   B. What is the effect of filtering on the properties of the three water samples?

      1. Filter **fresh** samples of solutions *A, B,* and *C* by slowly pouring each one through a separate funnel lined with a piece of filter paper. (See Figure 3-4.)

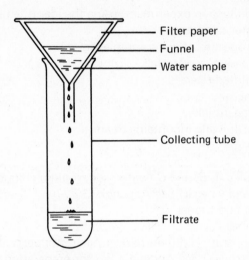

FIGURE 3-4
Filtration Apparatus

      2. Add these data to the table in Figure 3-3.

   C. What is the effect of filtering through filter paper and activated charcoal on the properties of the three water samples?

      1. Line a funnel with a piece of filter paper as shown in Figure 3-4, and slowly pour 3 cm of activated charcoal into the funnel. Now pour one of the water samples through the funnel.

      2. Repeat this procedure for the other two water samples, using a **fresh** piece of filter paper and fresh charcoal each time.

      3. Add these data to the table in Figure 3-3.

   D. What changes occur in the properties of the water samples after distillation?

      1. Place 100 ml of one of the original water samples into the distillation apparatus and boil for five minutes (see Appendix 3-3). Make observations of the physical properties of the *distillate* (the material in the jar) and add these data to the table in Figure 3-3. Repeat for the other samples.

      2. How do the properties of the distillate for each water sample compare with the original sample?

3. How do the initial properties of the three water samples compare with their properties after being boiled, filtered, or distilled?
4. What effect did each of these methods (boiling, filtering, or distillation) have on the removal of impurities from each of the water samples?
5. Based on all your observations in this investigation, identify a procedure for removing the greatest number of impurities from a water sample.
6. Using the procedure identified, purify a water sample composed of *equal parts* of samples *A, B,* and *C.*
7. How effective was the purification procedure?

E. Were any of the methods used in this investigation able to remove all the impurities from the water samples?

F. Infer the physical properties of water samples found:
1. At the base of a waterfall.
2. In a polluted river.
3. In the ocean.
4. In a stagnant lake.
5. In a fast flowing mountain stream.

Investigation Four

I. Objectives of this investigation
The student should be able to:
- A. Observe and list the properties of three water samples: after boiling and after filtering.
- B. Identify a procedure to determine the sudsing ability of three water samples.
- C. Compare the ability of three water samples to form suds.
- D. Compare the effects on the sudsing ability of water samples of boiling and filtering.
- E. Identify a procedure to determine the purity of a water sample.
- F. Plan and conduct an experiment using the identified procedure to determine the purity of a water sample.

II. Materials
- A. Three water samples* (distilled water, calcium bicarbonate or magnesium bicarbonate, calcium chloride or magnesium chloride)
- B. Soap solution* (20 ml)
- C. Detergent solution* (20 ml)
- D. Glass funnel
- E. Six sheets of filter paper
- F. Metric ruler
- G. Five test tubes
- H. Six beakers (250 ml)
- I. Medicine dropper

III. Procedure
- A. What are the properties of the three water samples?
  1. Observe and list the physical properties of the three water samples.
  2. List these data in the table in Figure 3-5.
  3. How do the properties of the three water samples compare?

Sample	Initially	After boiling	After filtering
A			
B			
C			

FIGURE 3-5
Physical Properties of the Water Samples

- B. What is the effect of boiling and filtering on the properties of the three water samples?
  1. Place 100 ml of each water sample in separate beakers and boil for three minutes.

*See Appendix 3-4: Preparation of the Water Samples and Soap and Detergent Solutions.

| | Height of suds in soap solution | | | Height of suds in detergent solution | | |
Sample	Initially	After boiling	After filtering	Initially	After boiling	After filtering
1						
2						
3						

FIGURE 3-6
Sudsing Ability of the Water Samples

2. Filter fresh portions of each water sample into a 250-ml beaker. (See Figure 3-4.)
3. How does each liquid, after being filtered or boiled, compare with the original sample? Add these data to the table in Figure 3-5.
4. Based on the properties that you have observed, how effective would you infer the techniques of boiling and filtering were for purifying each water sample?
5. **Save the boiled and filtered samples** of each of the three liquids for part D of this investigation.

C. Which of the three water samples will have the greatest sudsing ability?
1. Using the outline provided in the table in Figure 3-6, and a separate test tube for each sample, identify a procedure to determine the sudsing ability of the water samples with the *soap* solution.
2. Add these data to the table in Figure 3-6.
3. Repeat the procedure that you have identified with each of the water samples, **using fresh samples,** but this time use the *detergent* solution.
4. Add these data to the table in Figure 3-6.

D. What is the effect of boiling and filtering on the sudsing ability of the three water samples?
1. Using the boiled and filtered samples that you obtained in part B, determine the sudsing ability of these solutions using the soap and detergent solutions.
2. Add these data to the table in Figure 3-6.
3. Which technique, filtering or boiling, was the most effective in increasing the sudsing ability of the water samples? What observations did you make to support this conclusion?
4. Is the soap solution or the detergent solution the most effective for producing suds?

E. Referring to Investigation Three, what inferences can you make about the types of substances present in each of the three water samples?
1. How could the purity of a water sample be determined? Identify a procedure that could be used.
2. Plan and conduct an experiment, using the procedure identified, to determine the purity of ordinary tap water.

Investigation Five

I. Objectives of this investigation

The student should be able to:

A. Compare the properties of different acid solutions.

B. Compare the effects of different acid solutions on pieces of litmus paper, and on solutions of phenolphthalein, congo red, red cabbage juice, and grape juice.

C. Compare the effects of different acid solutions on pieces of zinc, marble, and aluminum.

D. Identify a procedure to determine whether a substance is an acid.

E. Plan and conduct an experiment, using the identified procedure, to determine whether a substance is an acid.

F. Identify a procedure to determine which of two acids is the stronger.

G. Plan and conduct an experiment, using the identified procedure, to determine which of two acids is the stronger.

II. Materials

A. Dilute solutions of the following*:
  1. Hydrochloric acid (100 ml)
  2. Sulfuric acid (100 ml)

B. Vinegar

C. Solution of five aspirin in 100 ml of distilled water

D. Lemon juice (100 ml)

E. Club soda (100 ml)

F. Red and blue litmus paper (10 strips each)

G. Congo red solution (20 ml)

H. Clear and red phenolphthalein solutions* (20 ml each)

I. Red cabbage juice and grape juice (20 ml each)

J. Pieces of marble, zinc, and aluminum

K. Medicine dropper and stirring rod

L. Six beakers (250 ml)

III. Procedure

A. What are the properties of acid solutions?

  1. Observe and record the physical properties, such as color, odor, and taste, of the following acids (use only the dilute solutions of items (a) and (b) and **do not taste** these two solutions):
     (a) Hydrochloric acid — **do not taste**
     (b) Sulfuric acid — **do not taste**
     (c) Vinegar
     (d) Aspirin solution
     (e) Lemon juice
     (f) Club soda

  2. What properties do all these solutions have in common? What proper-

*See Appendix 3-5: Preparation of Solutions.

36

ties are different? What other solutions have properties similar to those you have just observed?

B. What is the effect of the acid solutions on red and blue litmus paper and solutions of phenolphthalein, congo red, red cabbage juice, and grape juice?

1. Determine the effects of each of the acid solutions on each of these substances.

2. How does each acid solution compare in its reactions with litmus paper, phenolphthalein solutions, congo red, red cabbage juice, and grape juice?

3. How do these observations and comparisons compare with those made in part B of Investigation Six?

C. What is the effect of the acid solutions on samples of zinc, marble, and aluminum?

1. Determine the effects of each of the acid solutions on the pieces of zinc, marble, and aluminum.

2. How do the reactions of each of the acid solutions with the zinc, marble, and aluminum compare?

3. How do these observations and comparisons compare with those in part C in Investigation Six?

D. How can an acid be identified?

1. Based on all the observations and comparisons you have made in this investigation, identify a procedure to determine if a substance is an acid.

2. Plan and conduct an experiment, using the identified procedure, to determine whether ordinary tap water is an acid.

E. How can the strength of an acid be determined?

1. Identify a procedure you could use to determine which of two solutions is the stronger acid.

2. Plan and conduct an experiment, using the procedure identified, to determine whether vinegar or the aspirin solution is the stronger acid.

Investigation Six

I. Objectives of this investigation
The student should be able to:
A. Compare the properties of different basic solutions.
B. Compare the effects of different basic solutions on pieces of litmus paper and solutions of phenolphthalein, congo red, red cabbage juice, and grape juice.
C. Compare the effects of different basic solutions on pieces of marble, aluminum, and samples of grease.
D. Identify a procedure to determine whether a substance is basic.
E. Plan and conduct an experiment, using the identified procedure, to determine whether an unknown substance is basic.
F. Identify a procedure to determine which of two basic solutions is the stronger.
G. Plan and conduct an experiment, using the identified procedure, to determine which of two basic solutions is the stronger.

II. Materials
A. Dilute solutions of the following basic substances*:
   1. Calcium hydroxide (100 ml)
   2. Baking soda (sodium bicarbonate) (100 ml)
   3. Washing soda (sodium carbonate) (100 ml)
B. Household ammonia (100 ml)
C. Red and blue litmus paper (10 strips of each)
D. Clear and red phenolphthalein solutions† (20 ml each)
E. Congo red solution (20 ml)
F. Pieces of aluminum and marble
G. Red cabbage juice and grape juice (20 ml each)
H. Six pieces of glass spotted with grease (glass slides)
I. Six beakers (50 ml)
J. Ten test tubes
K. Potassium carbonate solution*

III. Procedure
A. What are the properties of basic solutions?
   1. Observe and record the physical properties of the following basic solutions:
     (a) Calcium hydroxide
     (b) Sodium bicarbonate
     (c) Sodium carbonate
     (d) Household ammonia
   2. What properties do all these substances have in common? How are they different?
B. What is the effect of the basic solutions on litmus paper, solutions of congo red, phenolphthalein, red cabbage juice, and grape juice?

*See Appendix 3-6: Preparation of the Basic Solutions.
†See Appendix 3-5.

    1. Determine the effects of the basic solutions on each of these substances. Carefully record all your observations.

    2. How do they compare in their reactions to the different substances?

    3. How do these observations and comparisons compare to those made in part B of Investigation Five?

C. What is the effect of the basic solutions on samples of marble and aluminum?

    1. Determine the effects of the basic solutions on both the marble and the aluminum.

    2. How do these observations and comparisons compare with those made in part C of Investigation Five?

D. What is the effect of basic solutions on grease stains?

    1. Place a small spot of grease, preferably meat fat, on a glass slide. Determine the effect of each of the basic solutions on this type of grease stain first by soaking, and then by rubbing. Again, carefully record all your observations.

    2. How do the basic solutions compare with water in their ability to remove the grease spots?

E. How can a basic solution be identified?

    1. Based on all the observations and comparisons, identify a procedure to determine if an unknown solution is basic.

    2. Plan and conduct an experiment, using the procedure identified, to determine if a solution of *potassium carbonate* is basic.

    3. What are the limitations of such a procedure?

    4. Identify a procedure to determine which of two basic solutions is the stronger.

    5. Plan and conduct an experiment, using the identified procedure, to determine if *sodium bicarbonate* or *household ammonia* is the stronger base.

Investigation Seven

I. Objectives of this investigation

The student should be able to:

A. Observe and list the properties of liquids formed by mixing together solutions of acids and bases.

B. Predict the effects of neutralized acid and base solutions on litmus paper, and solutions of phenolphthalein, congo red, red cabbage juice, and grape juice.

C. Verify the predictions concerning the effects of neutralized acid and base solutions on litmus paper, and solutions of phenolphthalein, congo red, red cabbage juice, and grape juice.

D. Predict the effects of neutralized acid and base solutions on pieces of marble, zinc, and aluminum.

E. Verify the predictions concerning the effects of neutralized acid and base solutions on pieces of marble, zinc, and aluminum.

F. Identify a procedure to determine whether a solution is neutral, that is, neither an acid nor a base.

G. Plan and conduct an experiment, using the identified procedure, to determine if a solution is neutral.

II. Materials

A. Solutions of the following acid and basic solutions*:
   1. Hydrochloric acid (75 ml)
   2. Sulfuric acid (75 ml)
   3. Calcium hydroxide (75 ml)
   4. Sodium hydroxide (75 ml)

B. Sodium chloride solution* (100 ml)

C. Red and blue litmus paper (10 strips of each)

D. Red and clear phenolphthalein solutionst (20 ml)

E. Congo red solution (20 ml)

F. Red cabbage juice and grape juice (20 ml)

G. Pieces of marble, zinc, and aluminum

H. Five test tubes

I. Four beakers (250 ml)

J. Graduated cylinder

K. Medicine dropper and stirring rod

III. Procedure

A. What are the properties of a solution resulting from a mixture of equal parts of an acid and a base? *Before beginning this investigation,* review your results from Investigations Five and Six.

   1. Carefully measure *exactly 30 ml* of hydrochloric acid and *exactly 30 ml* of sodium hydroxide solution. Clean the graduated cylinder thoroughly between measurings. *Slowly* pour the sodium hydroxide, a little at a time, into the hydrochloric acid while constantly stirring.

*See Appendix 3-7: Preparation of the Solutions.
†See Investigation Five for the preparation of these solutions.

40

2. What do you observe? How do the properties of the resulting solutions compare with the two original liquids?

3. Repeat the procedure described in step 1, using the following acids and bases:
   (a) *30 ml* of sulfuric acid and *30 ml* of calcium hydroxide
   (b) *30 ml* of hydrochloric acid and *30 ml* of calcium hydroxide
   (c) *30 ml* of sulfuric acid and *30 ml* of sodium hydroxide

4. How do each of the resulting solutions compare with the original two liquids? *Save these solutions.*

B. Predict the effects of the four solutions obtained in part A on litmus paper, phenolphthalein solutions, congo red, red cabbage juice, and grape juice.

1. Using part of each of the mixture solutions you obtained in part A, determine the effects of these solutions on each of the materials. *Use only small amounts of each solution for testing.*

2. Which of your predictions were supported by your observations?

C. Predict the effects of the solutions obtained in part A on samples of marble, zinc, and aluminum.

1. Determine the effects of each of the mixture solutions on the marble, zinc, and aluminum.

2. Which of your predictions were supported by your observations?

D. Based on all the observations and comparisons you have made in this investigation, identify a procedure for determining if a solution is neutral (neither an acid nor a base).

1. What are the limitations of such a procedure?

2. Plan and conduct an experiment, using the identified procedure, to determine if a salt (sodium chloride) solution is neutral.

Investigation Eight

I. Objectives of this investigation

The student should be able to:

A. Compare the changes that occur in identical strips of paper which are placed into several different solutions.

B. Compare the effects of several different types of paper placed into the same solution.

C. Identify the number of ingredients in an unknown solution.

D. Identify an unknown solution.

E. Predict changes that would occur in identical strips of paper placed into a mixture of several different solutions.

F. Plan and conduct an experiment to verify the prediction concerning the changes that would occur in identical strips of paper placed in a mixture of several different solutions.

II. Materials

A. Ten strips of varying texture paper (filter paper, glossy paper, smooth, newsprint, etc.) (approximately 2 X 20 cm)

B. Five test tubes (25 X 250 mm)

C. Metric ruler

D. Food coloring (red, blue, green, and yellow)

E. Chlorophyll solution*

F. Four solutions labeled 1, 2, 3, and 4[†] (food coloring, chlorophyll, and potassium permanganate)

G. Water

III. Procedure

A. How can the components of a mixture be separated and identified?

1. Add two drops of green and yellow food coloring to a test tube be containing 5 ml of water.

2. Place a 2 cm by 20 cm strip of filter paper into the test tube so that 1 to 2 cm is below the surface of the liquid. Attach the filter paper to the support with a paper clip or a thumb tack. (See Figure 3-7.)

3. Observe and record what happens each minute for ten minutes.

4. Repeat this procedure using the same solution and an identical piece of filter paper. How does this strip compare with the one produced in step 2?

B. How does the texture of the paper affect the results?

1. Determine what effect different types of paper have on the results you obtained in part A.

2. After several minutes, how does this paper compare with the strips produced in steps 2 and 3?

C. How can the number of ingredients in an unknown solution be identified?

1. Ask one of your classmates to give you samples (15 to 20 ml) of the four solutions (labeled 1, 2, 3, and 4) in separate and *unlabeled* test

---

*See part A-1 of Investigation Three, Conceptual Scheme I, for the preparation of this solution.
†See Appendix 3-8: Preparation of the Four Solutions.

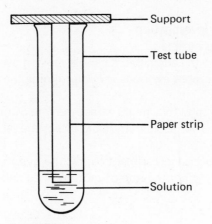

FIGURE 3-7
Paper Strip in Colored Solution

tubes. You should not know which solution is in each of the tubes. Using the apparatus described in step A-2, try and identify each of the solutions.

2. How do the properties of the four solutions compare? **Do not taste any of these solutions.** After ten minutes, how do the pieces of filter paper compare?
3. What inferences can you make concerning the number of ingredients present in each of the unlabeled test tubes?

D. How can you identify an unknown solution?
1. Ask one of your classmates to give you a test tube containing a 15-ml to 20-ml sample of a *mixture of two* of the four solutions labeled 1, 2, 3, and 4. You should not know which of the original solutions were mixed together.
2. Plan and conduct an experiment to determine the composition and number of ingredients of the unknown mixture.
3. After ten minutes in the solution, what do you predict a piece of filter paper would look like?

Investigation Nine

I. Objectives for this investigation
The student should be able to:
A. Observe and list the characteristics of a moving pendulum.
B. Identify one or more methods for determining the rate of motion of a pendulum.
C. Isolate the variables that might affect the rate of motion of a pendulum.
D. Hypothesize the variables that would affect the rate of motion of a pendulum.
E. Plan and conduct an experiment to test the hypotheses concerning the variables which affect the rate of motion of a pendulum.

II. Materials
A. Several pieces of string of varying size, thickness, and texture.
B. Assorted weights
C. Two paper cups
D. Two paper clips

III. Procedure
A. What are the characteristics of a moving pendulum?
  1. A pendulum is any weight or object suspended at the end of a string that is allowed to swing freely back and forth. Use a piece of string with a large paper clip or cup at the end in order to construct a pendulum. Add a small weight to the paper cup or attach a weight to the paper clip. Suspend the string by tying one end to a support, and set it swinging.
  2. Identify a method to determine the rate of motion of the pendulum, that is, how quickly or slowly it is swinging.
  3. Does the rate of motion of the pendulum remain the same or does it change?
B. How could the pendulum be made to swing faster or slower?
  1. Which variables do you hypothesize would affect the rate of motion of the pendulum?
  2. Plan and conduct an experiment in order to test the hypotheses concerning the variables that affect the rate of motion of the pendulum.
  3. What variables must be controlled? Which ones cannot be controlled?

Investigation Ten

I. Objectives of this investigation
The students should be able to:
A. Identify the materials which are, and are not, attracted by a magnet.
B. Classify materials attracted by a magnet according to their physical properties.
C. Identify the direction a freely turning bar magnet will point when it stops turning.
D. Identify the direction a compass needle will point when placed in an open area.
E. Compare the behavior of a suspended bar magnet with the behavior of a compass needle.
F. Hypothesize the relationship(s) between the behavior of a compass needle and that of a bar magnet.
G. Identify the poles of an unmarked magnet.

II. Materials
A. Bar magnet with N and S poles marked
B. Bar magnet with no poles marked
C. One piece of: wood, nickel, iron, glass, plastic, tin, rubber, copper, steel, sandpaper
D. Support from which a magnet can be freely suspended
E. String (2 m)
F. Compass

III. Procedure
A. What materials are attracted by a magnet? What materials are not attracted by a magnet?
   1. Touch one end of a bar magnet to a piece of wood. Place the word "wood" in the appropriate column in Figure 3-8.
   2. Repeat this procedure with each piece of material. Record all observations in Figure 3-8.
B. What are the physical properties of those materials attracted by a magnet?
   1. Place in one group those materials used in part A that were attracted by the magnet. Examine the physical properties of these pieces.

Materials attracted by a magnet	Materials not attracted by a magnet

FIGURE 3-8
Table for Interaction of Materials with a Magnet

III. Procedure (continued)

   Choose one property, such as color, shape, or size that some of these materials have in common. Divide the materials into two groups: one group of materials with the chosen property (group 1) and a second group without the chosen property (group 2).

   2. Select another property that some of the materials in group 1 have and the remainder of group 1 does not have. Repeat this same procedure for those materials in group 2; it may or may not be the same property that you used to separate group 1.

   3. Continue this method of classifying until each material is in a group by itself. Using the classification scheme developed in steps 1 to 3, describe the properties of each material attracted by a magnet.

C. In what direction will a freely turning bar magnet point when it stops turning?

   1. Within the classroom, identify the North, South, East, and West directions.

   2. Use a string to suspend a marked bar magnet from a support so that it turns freely. (See Figure 3-9.)

   3. After the magnet stops turning, in which direction is the end of the magnet marked "N" pointing?

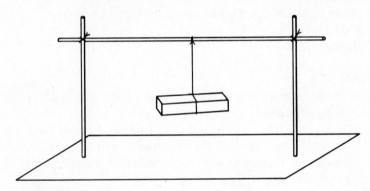

FIGURE 3-9
Suspended Bar Magnet

D. In which direction does a compass needle point when placed in an open area?

   1. In step C-1 the directions North, South, East, and West were identified.

   2. Examine the compass. One end of the compass needle may be pointed and marked with colored paint. This end should be used when determining the direction the compass needle is pointing.

   3. Place the compass on a level surface in the classroom away from any metal object. Be sure that the directions (N, S, E, W) printed on the compass coincide with the North, South, East, and West directions in the classroom.

   4. In which direction does the compass needle point?

5. Repeat steps 3 and 4, but place the compass on a level surface in different locations of the classroom. In which direction does the compass needle point in these locations?

E. Compare the behavior of a suspended bar magnet with the behavior of a compass needle.

F. Hypothesize a relationship between the behavior of a compass needle and that of a bar magnet.

G. How are the poles of an unmarked magnet identified? From your observations in parts A through F of this investigation, devise an identification scheme to distinguish one end of an *unmarked* bar magnet from the other end.

Investigation Eleven

I. **Objectives of this investigation**

The students should be able to:

A. Observe and record what happens to iron filings sprinkled on a piece of paper which is placed on top of a magnet.

B. Make inferences to explain observations of iron filings sprinkled on a piece of paper which is placed on top of a magnet.

C. Infer an explanation for the direction(s) a compass needle points when it is placed in various positions around the magnet.

D. Observe and record what happens to iron filings sprinkled on a piece of paper that has a current-carrying wire projecting through the center.

E. Make inferences to explain observations of iron filings placed on a piece of paper that has a current-carrying wire projecting through the center.

F. Predict the direction(s) a compass needle will point when brought close to a wire carrying an electric current.

G. Verify the predictions concerning the direction(s) a compass needle will point when brought close to a wire carrying an electric current.

H. Make inferences to explain the direction(s) a compass needle will point when brought close to a wire carrying an electric current.

I. Predict the position(s) of (1) iron filings and (2) a compass needle placed on a piece of paper over (1) a single loop of wire carrying an electric current and (2) a coil of wire carrying an electric current.

J. Verify the predictions concerning the position(s) of (1) iron filings and (2) a compass needle placed on a piece of paper over (1) a single loop of wire carrying an electric current and (2) a coil of wire carrying an electric current.

K. Make inferences to explain the position(s) of (1) iron filings and (2) a compass needle placed on a piece of paper over (1) a single loop of wire carrying an electric current and (2) a coil of wire carrying an electric current.

II. **Materials**

A. Iron filings (a salt shaker full)
B. Bar magnet
C. White paper or cardboard (8½ X 11 in.)
D. Small compass
E. Bell wire (several feet)
F. Dry cell (1½-volt)
G. Flashlight bulb and holder (type shown in Figure 3-10)
H. Electrical tape (1 roll)

III. **Procedure**

A. Is air the only thing that surrounds a magnet?

1. Place a bar magnet under a piece of plain white paper or cardboard. Sprinkle some iron filings as evenly as possible on top of the paper. Sketch your observations of the pattern formed by the iron filings. Compare your sketch with those of other members of the class. How do these sketches compare?

2. Keeping the magnet under the paper, slowly turn the magnet in a circle. Record your observations of the iron filings while the magnet is turning. When the magnet has been turned through half a circle, sketch what you observe.

3. Make inferences to explain your observations of the iron filings while the magnet is being turned.

4. Shake the iron filings back into their container. (Review Investigation Ten concerning the relationship between the behavior of a compass needle and the ends of a magnet.) Predict the direction(s) the compass needle will point when it is moved in various positions around the magnet. Verify your predictions.

5. Infer an explanation for the direction(s) the compass needle points when it is placed in various positions around the magnet.

6. Compare the data gathered when using the iron filings and the data gathered when using the compass. List the similarities and differences between the positions of the compass needle and the positions of iron filings when these objects are placed on a piece of paper covering a magnet.

B. What happens to iron filings when they are sprinkled on a piece of paper that has a current-carrying wire projecting through the center?

1. Mark the center of a piece of white paper or cardboard and put a small hole through this spot. Insert a long straight wire through the center of the small hole and perpendicular to the paper.

2. Connect a light bulb and holder, a dry cell, and the wire through the cardboard so that the bulb will light. (Investigation Twelve will help you to connect the light bulb and holder, dry cell, and wire.) Sprinkle some iron filings, as evenly as possible, on top of the paper. Sketch your observations of the pattern formed by the iron filings.

3. Make inferences to explain the observations of iron filings placed on a piece of paper that has a current-carrying wire projecting through the center.

4. Compare the observations and inferences made in part B with those made in part A.

C. What predictions can be made about the direction(s) a compass needle will point when brought close to a wire carrying an electric current?

1. Predict what will happen to a compass needle when it is brought close to the straight wire carrying an electric current that was connected in step B-2. Record your predictions.

2. Verify the predictions concerning the behavior of a compass needle brought close to a straight wire carrying an electric current.

3. Make inferences to explain the direction(s) a compass needle will point when brought close to a wire carrying an electric current.

D. What predictions can be made about iron filings and a compass needle brought near a loop of wire carrying an electric current?

1. Remove the straight length of wire from the paper in part C.

2. Shape this straight length of wire into a single loop of wire. Connect the loop to the battery and bulb as illustrated in Figure 3-10.

III. Procedure *(continued)*

3. Place a piece of white paper on top of the loop. Predict the position(s) of (a) iron filings and (b) a compass needle placed on the paper directly over the current-carrying loop of wire.

4. Verify the predictions concerning the position(s) of (a) iron filings and (b) a compass needle placed on the paper over a current-carrying loop of wire.

5. Make inferences to explain the position(s) of (a) iron filings and (b) a compass needle placed on the paper over a current-carrying loop of wire.

6. Compare the observations and inferences made in part C made with those in part D.

E. What will happen to iron filings and a compass needle placed on a piece of paper over a coil of wire carrying an electric current?

1. Twist the wire loop used in part D into many loops, side by side. Hold the loops together with tape. This is a coil of wire. Connect the coil to the battery and bulb as illustrated in Figure 3-11.

FIGURE 3-10
Loop of Wire Connected to a Battery and Bulb

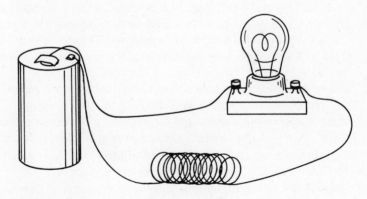

FIGURE 3-11
Coil of Wire Connected to a Battery and Bulb

2. Place a piece of white paper on top of the coil. From the data col-
    lected in part D, predict what will happen to iron filings and a compass
    needle brought near this current-carrying coil of wire. Verify your
    predictions.
3. Make inferences to explain the direction(s) a compass needle will
    point and the pattern(s) the iron filings will make when brought close
    to a current-carrying coil of wire.
4. Compare your inferences and observations made in each part of this
    investigation. What, other than air, surrounds a magnet and various
    shaped wires carrying an electric current.

Investigation Twelve

I. Objectives of this investigation
The students should be able to:

A. Predict the way(s) one flashlight bulb, one wire, and a dry cell can be connected so that the bulb will light.

B. Verify the predictions concerning the way(s) one flashlight bulb, one wire, and one dry cell can be connected so that the bulb will light.

C. Infer the path taken by electricity to light a flashlight bulb when one wire and a dry cell are used.

D. Predict the way(s) one flashlight bulb and holder, two wires, and a dry cell can be connected so that the bulb will light.

E. Verify the predictions concerning the way(s) one flashlight bulb and holder, two wires, and a dry cell can be connected so that the bulb will light.

F. Infer the path taken by electricity to light a flashlight bulb when two wires and one dry cell are used.

II. Materials
A. Flashlight bulb

B. Dry cell (1½-volt)

C. Bell wire (several feet)

D. Flashlight bulb holder (type shown in Figure 3-10)

III. Procedure
A. How can a dry cell and one wire be connected in order to light a flashlight bulb?

1. Examine a piece of wire, a flashlight bulb, and a dry cell. Draw diagrams predicting the way(s) the flashlight bulb, dry cell, and wire can be connected so that the bulb will light. (See Figure 3-12 for the symbols to use in your diagrams.)

2. Verify your predictions by connecting the wire, flashlight bulb, and dry cell as pictured in your diagrams.

 Wire

 Bulb

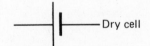 Dry cell

FIGURE 3-12
Symbols for Electrical Diagrams

3. Examine the inaccurate diagrams. Change the part(s) of each inaccu-
    rate diagram that was responsible for the inaccuracy. Now set up the
    pieces of equipment in order to verify the corrected diagrams.
4. Infer the path taken by the electricity in order to light the bulb.

B. How can a dry cell, two pieces of wire, and a flashlight bulb be connected
    so that the bulb will light?
1. Examine the dry cell, two pieces of wire, and a flashlight bulb in a
    holder. Draw diagrams predicting the way(s) the flashlight bulb, dry
    cell, and wires can be connected so that the bulb will light. Use the
    same symbols as in Figure 3-12.
2. Verify your predictions by connecting the equipment as pictured in
    each diagram.
3. Examine the diagrams that were accurate predictions and those that
    were inaccurate predictions.
4. Change the part(s) of each inaccurate diagram to make it accurate.
    Verify your new prediction.
5. Infer the path taken by the electricity in order to light the bulb.

Investigation Thirteen

I. Objectives of this investigation

The students should be able to:

A. Predict the way(s) two flashlight bulbs, two wires, and a dry cell can be connected so that the bulbs will light.

B. Verify the prediction(s) concerning the way(s) two flashlight bulbs, two wires, and a dry cell can be connected so that the bulb will light.

C. Predict the way(s) one end of a wire can be disconnected causing one and then two flashlight bulbs to go out.

D. Verify the predictions concerning the way(s) one end of a wire can be disconnected so that one and then two flashlight bulbs will go out.

E. Predict the way(s) two flashlight bulbs, three wires, and a dry cell can be connected so that the bulbs will light.

F. Verify the predictions concerning the way(s) two flashlight bulbs, three wires, and a dry cell can be connected so that the bulbs will light.

G. Predict the way(s) two flashlight bulbs, four wires, and a dry cell can be connected so that the bulbs will light.

H. Verify the predictions concerning the way(s) two flashlight bulbs, four wires, and a dry cell can be connected so that the bulbs will light.

I. Compare the properties of two lighted flashlight bulbs when they are both connected to a dry cell by two, three, and four wires.

J. Hypothesize a cause for inconsistent results among classmates concerning the observed properties of two lighted flashlight bulbs.

K. Isolate the variables which caused inconsistencies among classmates concerning the observed properties of two lighted bulbs.

L. Plan and conduct an experiment to determine the cause of inconsistent results among classmates concerning the observed properties of two lighted bulbs.

M. Infer an explanation for the properties of two lighted flashlight bulbs connected to a dry cell by two, three, and four wires.

II. Materials

A. Two flashlight bulbs in holders (type shown in Figure 3-10)

B. Dry cell (1½-volt)

C. Bell wire (several feet)

III. Procedure

A. How can a dry cell and two wires be connected in order to light two bulbs?

1. (See Investigation Ten, and connect one bulb and holder, two wires, and a dry cell so that the bulb will light.) Draw diagram(s) predicting the way(s) a second bulb and holder can be added to the equipment so that both bulbs will light.

2. Verify your predictions.

3. Note the diagram(s) that were accurate predictions. Examine the inaccurate predictions. Change the part(s) of each diagram showing in-

accurate predictions so that both bulbs will light. Verify your cor-
rected predictions.

4.   Examine all your diagrams that indicate the way(s) that the equipment can be connected such that both bulbs will light. Predict the
place(s) where (1) *one* end of a wire can be disconnected causing
only one of the two bulbs to go out, and where (2) *one* end of a wire
can be disconnected causing both bulbs to go out. Verify your predictions.

B.   How can a dry cell and three wires be connected together to light two
flashlight bulbs?

1.   Draw diagram(s) predicting the way(s) a dry cell and three wires can
be connected together so that two flashlight bulbs in holders will
light.

2.   Verify your predictions by connecting the flashlight bulbs, the dry
cell, and the three wires as pictured in each of your diagrams.

3.   Note the diagram(s) that were accurate predictions. Examine the inaccurate predictions. Change the part(s) of each diagram showing inaccurate predictions so that both bulbs will light. Verify your cor-
rected predictions.

C.   How can a dry cell and four wires be used to light two bulbs? Repeat the
procedure in steps B-1 to B-3 using four wires.

D.   Compare the observed properties of two lighted flashlight bulbs when
they are connected together with a dry cell and two wires, three wires,
and four wires. Discuss your list of observed properties with your classmates to determine if all lists are the same. Hypothesize a cause for any
inconsistencies among lists.

1.   Isolate the variables which caused inconsistencies among classmates
concerning the observed properties of two lighted bulbs.

2.   Plan and conduct an experiment to determine the cause of inconsistencies among the observed properties of two lighted bulbs.

E.   Infer an explanation for the properties of two lighted flashlight bulbs
when they are both connected to a dry cell by two, three, and four
wires.

CONCEPTUAL SCHEME IV

Living Organisms Are a Product of Heredity and Environment

Investigation One

I. Objectives of this investigation

The student should be able to:

A. Compare the characteristics of seeds.
B. Compare the germination times of seeds.
C. Identify the location(s) of growth in the leaf and stem of a plant.
D. Predict the location(s) of growth in the root of a plant.
E. Verify the prediction of location(s) of growth in the root of a plant.
F. Infer the location(s) of growth in a tree.

II. Materials

A. Seeds: corn, radish, wheat, mung, sunflower, pea (about 15 of each seed used)
B. Hand lens
C. Single-edged razor blade
D. Small jar
E. Water
F. Vermiculite or soil (enough to fill each paper cup used)
G. One paper cup for each kind of seed (with holes in the bottom made with darning needles) on a small container to catch water
H. Toothpick
I. India ink
J. Metric ruler
K. Paper towels
L. Closed container (such as a Petri dish or a small jar with a lid)

III. Procedure

A. What characteristics do seeds have in common? How are seeds different?
   1. Examine some seeds. Use a hand lens in order to observe all the characteristics of the seeds.
   2. Use a single-edged razor blade to open some of the seeds. What do you observe inside of the seeds?
   3. Place some seeds in a small jar, add water, and soak them for 24

56

hours. Open some of these seeds. Is there anything different between a soaked and an unsoaked seed? How do you explain this difference based on Investigation Five, Conceptual Scheme I?

B. Do the same kinds of seeds, planted at the same time, germinate at the same time? Do different kinds of seeds germinate at different times? Do plants grow the same amount each day?

1. Put vermiculite or soil in the paper cups (use a separate cup for each kind of seed).
2. Place some seeds in each cup, about 15 mm below the surface of the vermiculite or soil. Why is it important to keep a record of the number of seeds planted?
3. Put the same amount of water in each cup and place the cup on a container to catch the water.
4. Put your name, date, and the kind of seed planted on each cup used.
5. Keep accurate records by completing a table, such as in Figure 4-1.

C. Where does the growth occur in a plant? Where does the growth occur in a stem? Where does it occur in a leaf? Does growth occur in different places in different plants?

1. After the plants in part B emerge, place small marks equal distances apart on the stems and the leaves. Use a toothpick dipped in India ink to make your marks. Record the distance between the marks.
2. Why is it important that the marks be an equal distance apart?
3. Observe the plants over a period of time and identify the location(s) of growth in the leaf and stem of the plants.

D. Where does the growth occur in a root? Does growth occur at the same place in the roots of different kinds of plants? Do all parts of the root grow at the same rate?

1. Plan an investigation to verify your prediction concerning the location of growth in the root of plants.
2. Root growth can be studied if seeds are placed on dampened paper towels and kept in a closed container (such as a Petri dish or a small jar with a lid).

E. Trees get bigger every year. Based on the data collected in this investigation, infer what part(s) of the tree grow(s).

Kind and number of seeds	Date planted	Date each plant emerged	Height of each plant the second day	Height of plant the third day	Fourth day

FIGURE 4-1
Table for Growth of Plants

Investigation Two

I. Objectives of this investigation
The student should be able to:
A. Observe and list the characteristics of mold on bread.
B. Isolate the variables that will affect the growth of mold on bread.
C. Identify a procedure to measure the amount of mold growth on bread.
D. Plan and conduct an experiment to determine which variables will affect the growth of mold on bread.

II. Materials
A. Moldy bread*: bakery bread, water, jar with a lid
B. Tweezers
C. Pot holder
D. At least 3 jars, with lids
E. Water
F. Bunsen burner, candle, or alcohol lamp

III. Procedure
A. What variables in the environment will cause a slice of bread to develop mold? What environmental variables will cause the greatest growth of bread mold?
   1. Observe and list the characteristics of mold on a slice of bread.
   2. List the environmental variables that were present when the slice of bread developed mold.
B. Plan and conduct an experiment to determine which environmental variables will cause the greatest amount of mold growth on a slice of bread and will also affect the other characteristics of mold.
   1. Mold can be transferred from one slice of bread to another slice of bread. (See Appendix 4-2: Directions for Transferring Mold from One Slice of Bread to Another Slice of Bread).
   2. Only one environmental variable can be studied at one time; all the other variables must be held constant in order to have a controlled experiment.
   3. Identify a procedure to measure the amount of mold growth on a slice of bread.
   4. Keep accurate records regarding your experiment, such as the date and time started, variable being studied, variables held constant, amount of mold growth, and other characteristics of the mold.

*See Appendix 4-1: Directions for Producing Mold Growth on a Slice of Bread.

Investigation Three

I. Objectives of this investigation

The student should be able to:

A. Observe and describe the various structures of a flower.

B. Infer from observations of a flower, a function for each of its structures.

C. Compare albino corn seeds.

D. Predict the characteristics of the plants that will germinate from corn seeds.

E. Verify the predictions of the characteristics of the plants that will germinate from corn seeds.

F. Make inferences regarding the causes for the characteristics of corn plants.

II. Materials

A. Various flowers

B. Three albino corn seeds (can be purchased from a biological supply house)

C. Vermiculite or soil (to fill paper cup)

D. Paper cup (with holes in the bottom made with darning needles)

E. Single-edged razor blade

III. Procedure

A. Which structures are found in all flowers? What is the function of each of the structures of the flower?

1. Examine different kinds of flowers. Describe the structures of each flower and identify those structures that are similar from flower to flower. Identify those structures of each flower that cannot be found in the other flowers you examined.

2. Use a single-edged razor blade to cut open the center part of different flowers. Describe the structure on the inside of the flowers. How do the inside structures of these flowers compare with each other? List the similarities and differences.

3. The purpose of a flower is to produce seeds. What inferences can you make regarding the function of the various structures of the flower?

B. When corn seeds germinate, how are the plants similar and how are they different?

1. Examine the albino corn seeds. How are they similar? How are they different from each other?

2. Predict what the corn plants will look like that will germinate from these seeds.

3. Put vermiculite or soil in a paper cup.

4. Place three corn seeds in each cup, about 15 mm below the surface of the vermiculite.

5. Put some water in the cup and place the cup in a container.

6. Label the cup with your name and the date that the seeds were planted.

III. Procedure *(continued)*

7. After the seeds germinate, how does your prediction regarding the characteristics of the corn plants and the actual characteristics of the corn plants compare?

C. What inferences can you make regarding the characteristics of the corn plants?

Investigation Four

I. Objectives of this investigation
The student should be able to:
- A. Observe and draw the component parts (cells) of different living organisms, using a microscope.
- B. Compare the cells from the same and from different living organisms.

II. Materials
- A. Microscope (100X power)
- B. Microscope slide and cover slip
- C. Onion
- D. Toothpick
- E. Safranin or methylene blue stain (4 or 5 drops)
- F. Medicine dropper
- G. Water
- H. Single-edged razor blade

III. Procedure
- A. How do the various parts of an onion compare?
  1. Remove the outer leaves from an onion. Gently remove a thin layer of "skin" from the inner leaves. Put this "skin" on a microscope slide, add a drop of water, and cover with a cover slip.
  2. Observe the onion "skin" with a microscope. Sketch what you observe.
  3. Without removing the cover slip, put a drop of stain (safranin or methylene blue) at the edge of the cover slip. How do your observations of the onion "skin" compare now with those that you made prior to adding the stain? Sketch what you observe and then clean the slide and cover slip.
  4. Take a section out of the inside of the onion. Use a razor blade to make a very thin slice lengthwise through this section. Using this thin slice, prepare another microscope slide. Stain the onion slice, using the same procedure used in step 3, and examine it with the microscope. Sketch what you observe and then clean the slide and cover slip.
  5. List the characteristics that this sketch has in common with the sketch you made of the stained "skin."
  6. These sketches of various parts of the onion are of cells, the component part of living organisms. How are onion cells taken from different places in the onion alike and different?
- B. How do the cells from your body compare with the cells from an onion?
  1. Gently scrape the inside surface of your cheek with a clean toothpick. Wipe the toothpick on a microscope slide, add a drop of water and a drop of stain, and cover with a cover slip. Observe the cells from inside your cheek. Sketch your observations and then clean the slide and cover slip.
  2. If someone in your class has been sunburned, a layer of cells will

III.   Procedure *(continued)*

easily peel off their body. Prepare a microscope slide of this skin, stain the skin, and examine it under a microscope. Sketch your observations and then clean the slide and cover slip.

3.   How are the cheek cells and the skin cells alike and how are they different?

C.   How are the cells from an onion and from your body similar? How are they different? Observe all the sketches made in this investigation in order to answer these questions.

Investigation Five

I. Objectives of this investigation

The student should be able to:
A. Prepare a *Euglena* culture.
B. Observe and draw *Euglena,* using a microscope.
C. Identify a procedure to measure the size of an individual *Euglena*.
D. Observe and describe the method of reproduction used by *Euglena*.
E. Identify a procedure to measure the rate of reproduction for *Euglena*.
F. Isolate the variables that affect the behavior of *Euglena*.
G. Plan and conduct an experiment to determine which variables affect the behavior of *Euglena*.

II. Materials

A. Glass jar
B. Distilled water (to fill glass jar)
C. Heat source
D. Wheat, rice, or timothy kernels
E. *Euglena* culture
F. Microscope (100X power)
G. Microscope slide
H. Medicine dropper

III. Procedure

A. Prepare a culture of *Euglena*. (See Appendix 4-3: Preparation of a *Euglena* Culture.)
B. What observations can you make about the *Euglena*? Place a few drops of the *Euglena* culture on a clean microscope slide; a cover slip is not necessary. Observe the *Euglena* culture under the low power objective of the microscope. Sketch a *Euglena*.
C. How big are *Euglena*? How do they compare with each other in size? Identify a procedure to measure the size of a *Euglena*. Measurement can be in units other than inches or centimeters. What could you put on the microscope slide in order to compare the size of the *Euglena*?
D. How do *Euglena* reproduce? Place some *Euglena* from your culture on a clean microscope slide. Observe these living organisms with a microscope and try to see them reproduce. Describe the method of reproduction used by *Euglena*. Identify a procedure to measure the rate of reproduction for *Euglena*.
E. How do *Euglena* behave in sunlight and in darkness? How do *Euglena* behave in cold water as compared with warm water? What kind of food do *Euglena* prefer to eat?
   1. Isolate the variables that may affect the behavior of *Euglena*.
   2. Plan and conduct an experiment to determine which variables will affect the behavior of *Euglena*.

Investigation Six

I. Objectives of this investigation

The student should be able to:

A. Observe and list the characteristics of a colony of bacteria.

B. Infer an explanation for the number of colonies of bacteria growing on an inoculated Petri dish.

C. Compare the number of colonies of bacteria growing on Petri dishes inoculated with various materials.

D. Infer an explanation for the differences in the number of colonies of bacteria on Petri dishes inoculated with various materials.

E. Hypothesize methods of inhibiting the growth of bacteria.

F. Plan and conduct an experiment to determine: (1) environmental conditions that will inhibit the growth of bacteria and (2) chemical substance that will inhibit the growth of bacteria.

G. Infer methods of preventing an infection caused by bacteria.

II. Materials

A. Nutrient media*

B. Source of heat (for example, a hot plate)

C. Three sterilized Petri dishes†

D. Container for cooking (such as a metal pot)

E. Labels

F. Transparent tape

III. Procedure

A. How are bacterial colonies (groups of bacteria) similar in appearance and how are they different?

1. Prepare containers for the growth of bacteria. (See Appendixes 4-4 and 4-5: Preparation of Media to Provide the Nourishment for the Bacteria and Preparation of Containers for the Growth of Bacteria.)

2. Inoculate your Petri dish by opening the dish very slightly, touch the media with one of your fingers, and close the dish quickly. Seal the dish with a piece of transparent tape. Keep the dish sealed during the remainder of this investigation.‡

3. Put the dish in a warm, dark place. Observe your inoculated Petri dish a week later. Individual bacteria cannot be seen without a microscope; however, they can be seen as a colony. What shape, size, and color are each of the colonies? Record your observations and make a sketch of the colony growth.

*See Appendix 4-4: Preparation of Media to Provide the Nourishment for the Bacteria.
†See Appendix 4-5: Preparation of Containers for the Growth of Bacteria.
‡**Caution:** Some bacteria can be dangerous. During this investigation, an inoculated Petri dish should not be opened. To prevent a dish from accidentally opening, seal the top and bottom together with a piece of transparent tape. Bacteria should only be observed through the cover of the Petri dish. When you are through with the Petri dish, boil it in water for at least one-half hour. The disposable dishes can then be thrown away and the glass dishes can be cleaned out before storing them for future use.

4. Discuss your observations with the other students in your class. List those characteristics that the colonies have in common and those characteristics that differ from colony to colony.
5. How do the number of bacterial colonies compare in different Petri dishes? What explanation can you give for the number of bacterial colonies in each Petri dish?

B. Where are bacteria found? What places have the most bacteria? What places have the fewest bacteria?
1. Inoculate one Petri dish with one object. For example, touch it with a coin, your comb, toothbrush, fork, let a fly walk across the media, comb your hair over it, or just expose the media to the air for about ten minutes. There should be one Petri dish in the classroom that is left unopened as a control. Why is this control necessary?
2. Label each dish with your name and the object used to inoculate it. Put each dish in a warm, dark place for a week. Observe the colonies of bacteria. Compare your dish with the dishes inoculated by the other students.
3. Count the number of colonies in each Petri dish. Rank the Petri dishes according to the number of colonies found in each dish. Which objects caused the growth of more colonies? Which objects caused the growth of fewer colonies? Infer an explanation for the differences in the number of colonies of bacteria on the Petri dishes.

C. What environmental conditions will inhibit the growth of bacteria? What chemical substances will inhibit the growth of bacteria?
1. Discuss these questions with the members of your class. Identify the factors that you believe will inhibit the growth of bacteria. Separate these factors into two groups: environmental factors and chemical factors. Which of these factors are both environmental and chemical? Select one of these factors to investigate. Plan and conduct an experiment to determine the effect of this factor on the growth of the bacteria colonies.
2. During the next week, observe the results. Compare your results with those obtained by the other members of your class. Which factors are the best inhibitors of bacterial growth?

D. Based on data collected in this investigation, infer methods of preventing a bacterial infection.

Investigation Seven

I. Objectives of this investigation
The student should be able to:
- A. Classify all the students in the classroom who can and cannot taste the chemical on a piece of PTC paper.
- B. Formulate an hypothesis to explain why some students can, and other students cannot, taste the chemical on a piece of PTC paper.
- C. Plan and conduct an experiment regarding the ability of some students to taste the chemical on a piece of PTC paper.
- D. Make predictions regarding the ability of other people to taste the chemical on a piece of PTC paper.

II. Materials
- A. Vial of PTC paper (available from a biological supply house)

III. Procedure
- A. Which students can taste the chemical on a piece of PTC paper?
    1. Place a piece of PTC paper on the tip of your tongue. This paper contains a harmless chemical known as phenythiocarbamide. Describe the taste of the PTC paper. Which students can taste something bitter and which students cannot?
    2. Classify the students into two categories: those who taste something bitter and those who cannot taste anything bitter. What other characteristics do the students in each group have in common?
    3. Why can some students taste the chemical on a piece of PTC paper as being bitter, while other students cannot?
- B. Your answer to the question: "Why can some students taste the chemical on a piece of PTC paper as being bitter, while other students cannot?" is an hypothesis. Plan and conduct an experiment to test your hypothesis.
- C. Based on data you have collected from this investigation, predict the ability of other members of your family to taste or not to taste the chemical on a piece of PTC paper. To accurately predict is additional support for your hypothesis.

Investigation Eight

I. Objectives of this investigation

The student should be able to:

A. Compare the characteristics of fruit flies *(Drosophila).*
B. Formulate an hypothesis to explain the characteristics of the offspring resulting from the mating of selected fruit flies.
C. Plan and conduct an experiment to determine the characteristics of the offspring resulting from the mating of selected fruit flies.
D. Infer an explanation for the similarities and differences of children with their parents.

II. Materials

A. Bananas
B. Hand lens
C. *Drosophila melanogaster* (fruit fly): red eye stock and a white eye stock, or normal wing stock and a vestigial wing stock*
D. Quart milk bottles (at least 2)
E. Sterilized, absorbent cotton (enough to plug all the bottles used)
F. A minimum of 12 small bottles (such as baby food jars) (one bottle should have a tight fitting lid)
G. Media (can be obtained from a biological supply house) (enough for a depth of 5 cm in the 2-qt milk bottles and 2 cm in 10 of the small bottles)
H. Metal can covered with nylon mesh
I. Ice and water
J. Petri dish

III. Procedure

A. How are fruit flies similar in appearance and how are they different?
   1. Put some very ripe bananas in a dish and allow them to stand open. A culture of wild fruit flies should breed on the bananas. Immobilize some of the fruit flies (see Appendix 4-6: Immobilizing Flies) and observe them with a hand lens.
   2. What characteristics do the wild fruit flies have in common? How are the fruit flies different?
   3. Distinguish between the female and the male fruit flies. (See Appendix 4-7: Techniques for Working with Fruit Flies). Draw a picture of a wild female fruit fly and a wild male fruit fly.
B. If wild fruit flies are mated, what will the offspring look like?
   1. Mate a wild female fruit fly and a wild male fruit fly, following the directions in the Appendixes 4-6 and 4-7: Immobilizing Flies and Techniques for Working with Fruit Flies.
   2. Identify the characteristics that the offspring share and do not share with their parents.
   3. Classify the offspring according to their appearances. Count and

*These types can be purchased from a biological supply house. Order two stocks: red eye and white eye *or* normal wing and vestigial wing.

III. **Procedure** *(continued)*

record the number of offspring in each classified group.

4. Count and record the number of male offspring and the number of female offspring.

5. If you mated the offspring, what would their offspring look like? What percentage of the offspring would be males? Females? Verify your predictions by doing an experiment.

C. If you mate a long-winged fruit fly with a vestigial-winged fruit fly, what will the offspring look like? (*Or:* If you mate a red-eyed fruit fly with a white-eyed fruit fly, what will the offspring look like?)

1. Examine the long-winged and vestigial-winged fruit flies (or red-eyed and white-eyed fruit flies). Use a hand lens to distinguish their characteristics. How are these flies similar and how are they different? Are these flies different in any way from the wild flies you examined in part A? State the way(s) in which they are different.

2. Formulate an hypothesis to explain the characteristics of the offspring resulting from the mating of these fruit flies.

3. Test your hypothesis by planning and conducting an experiment to determine the characteristics of the offspring resulting from the mating of the following fruit flies:

   (a) Normal wing and normal wing (or red eye and red eye)

   (b) Vestigial wing and vestigial wing (or white eye and white eye)

   (c) Normal wing female and vestigial wing male (or red eye female and white eye male)

   (d) Normal wing male and vestigial wing female (or red eye male and white eye female)

4. Keep accurate records on the offspring, including the number of normal-winged (or red-eyed) flies, vestigial-winged (or white-eyed) flies, male flies, and female flies.

5. If you mated the offspring from the crosses in step 3, what would their offspring look like? Test your predictions. Your data should include the number of vestigial-winged (or white-eyed) males and females, normal-winged (or red-eyed) males and females, total vestigial (or white-eyed) flies, total normal winged (or red-eyed) flies, total male, and total female flies. Record your data and compare the results. .

D. Why do you look like your parents? Infer an explanation for the similarities and differences of children with their parents.

The Physical Universe, and All Systems in It, Are CONCEPTUAL Constantly Changing SCHEME

V

Investigation One

I. Objectives of this investigation

The students should be able to:
A. Identify the direction(s) light travels from a light bulb.
B. Infer the direction of travel of a beam of light from a bulb.
C. Graph the area lighted by a bulb against the distance between the bulb and that area.
D. Use a graph to predict the area lighted when a bulb is placed at different distances from that area.
E. Verify the predictions of the area lighted when a bulb is placed at different distances from that area.

II. Materials

A. Light bulb and holder (type shown in Figure 3-10)
B. Dry cell (1½-volt)
C. Bell wire (several feet)
D. Two chalkboard erasers
E. Black construction paper (5 X 5 in. piece with hole in center)
F. Clay (1 package)
G. Index card (white, 5 X 7 in.)

III. Procedure

A. In what direction(s) does light from a bulb travel?
1. Connect a light bulb and holder, a dry cell, and two long pieces of bell wire so that the bulb will light. (See Investigation Twelve, Conceptual Scheme III, for a method of connecting the above pieces of equipment so that the bulb will light.)
2. Hold the chalkboard erasers above the bulb and lightly clap them together. How does the chalk dust help you to answer the question, "In what direction(s) does light from a bulb travel?" (A dark room will produce the best results.)
3. Infer the direction of travel of a single beam of light from the bulb.

B. What happens to the size and shape of a spot of light on a screen when the screen is moved away from and closer to a light source?

1. Cut a 5-in. square from black construction paper. There should be a small hole about the size of a pencil eraser in the center of the black paper. Use a piece of clay to support this square in front of the light bulb and holder used in part A. Line up the hole with the light bulb.

2. On a white index card (5 X 7 in.) rule off ¼-in. squares. Support this white card with a piece of clay. This card will be used as a screen upon which the light from the bulb can be projected. Place the screen, the black paper, and the light bulb in a straight line so that a beam of light passes through the hole and falls on the screen. (See Figure 5-1.)

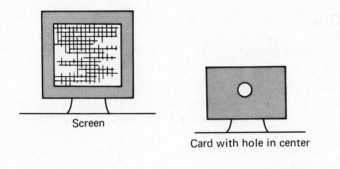

Screen

Card with hole in center

Light source

FIGURE 5-1
Position of Screen, Hole, and Light Bulb

3. Have a distance of 10 cm between the screen and the black paper, and between the black paper and the bulb.

4. Connect the light bulb to the dry cell. Look over the top of the black paper and count the number of squares on the screen that are lighted. Record this number and the distance between the screen and flashlight bulb (20 cm).

5. Move the screen about 2 cm farther away from the light bulb. Again look over the black paper and count the number of squares on the screen that are lighted. Record this number and also the distance between the screen and the bulb. How does the brightness of the light on the screen compare with the brightness observed in step 4?

6. Repeat the procedure used in steps 4 and 5 several more times— moving the screen closer to the light as well as farther away.

7. Graph the data gathered above, plotting the area lighted on the screen by the bulb (that is, the number of squares) against the distance from the bulb. (See Figure 5-2.)

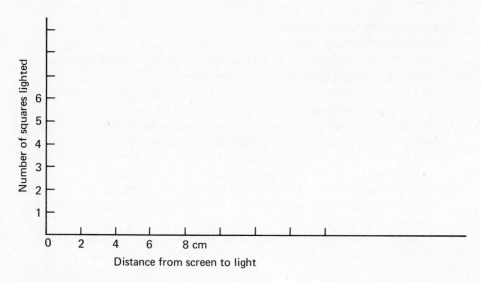

FIGURE 5-2
Graph of Area Lighted by a Bulb

C. Use the graph to predict the area that would be lighted when a bulb is placed at different distances from the screen.
D. Verify the predictions of the area lighted when a bulb is placed at different distances from the screen.

Investigation Two

I. Objectives of this investigation
The students should be able to:
A. Identify the color projected on a screen when pieces of cellophane are placed between a light source and the screen.
B. Predict the color that will be projected on a screen when the screen and the cellophane are the same color.
C. Verify your prediction concerning the color projected on the screen when the screen and the cellophane are the same color.
D. Predict the color to be projected on a screen when the screen and the cellophane are different colors; the screen not being white.
E. Verify your predictions concerning the color projected on a screen when the screen and the cellophane are different colors (the screen not being white).
F. Formulate inferences to explain why objects appear to be of different colors.

II. Materials
A. Two index cards (5 X 7 in., white)
B. Clay (1 package)
C. Seven-inch square of black construction paper with hole in center
D. Three-inch squares of cellophane (blue, green, yellow, red, clear)
E. Cellophane tape
F. Light bulb and holder (type shown in Figure 3-10)
G. Dry cell (1½-volt)
H. One piece of red, yellow, green, and blue construction paper (5 X 7 in.) screens

III. Procedure
A. What similarities and differences are there between the color of a piece of cellophane and color of light projected through the cellophane onto a screen?
1. Place a 5 X 7 in. white index card on a piece of clay, so that the card stands up straight. This card will be used as a screen.
2. In the center of a 7-in. square of black construction paper, place a small hole about the size of a pencil-top eraser. Stand this card up on a piece of clay.
3. In the center of a 5 X 7 in. white index card, cut out a 1-in. square. Tape a piece of colored cellophane over the hole in the index card. Place this card on a clay stand.
4. Place the index card screen, colored cellophane square, and the paper with the small hole in a straight line in front of a light bulb and holder. (See Figure 5-3). There should be about 10 cm between each object.
5. Connect the light bulb and holder to a dry cell (see Investigation Twelve, Conceptual Scheme III) so that the bulb is lighted. Identify and record the color projected on the screen and the color of the cellophane.

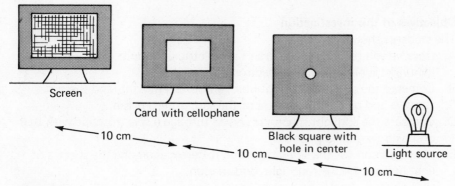

Screen

Card with cellophane

10 cm

Black square with
hole in center

10 cm

Light source

10 cm

FIGURE 5-3
Position of Screen, Cellophane, Black Square with Small Hole, and Bulb

      6.   Repeat steps 4 and 5, using a different piece of cellophane each time. Complete the table in Figure 5-4.

  B. How will the color projected on a screen appear if colored screens are used?

      1.   Predict the color that will be projected on the screen when the screen and the cellophane are the same color.

      2.   Verify the predictions concerning the color projected on the screen when the screen and cellophane are the same color. Replace the white index card screen in part A with various colored 5 X 7 in. pieces of construction paper.

      3.   Predict the color that will be projected on the screen when the screen and the cellophane are different colors (the screen not being white).

      4.   Verify your predictions concerning the color projected on the screen when the screen and the cellophane are different colors (the screen not being white).

  C. Formulate inferences to explain why objects appear to be of different colors.

Color of cellophane	Color of spot on the screen
Red	
Yellow	
Green	
Blue	
Clear	
Red-yellow*	
Red-blue*	
Red-green*	
Yellow-green*	
Yellow-blue*	
Green-blue*	

*Two different pieces of colored cellophane are taped together.

FIGURE 5-4
Table for Colors Projected on a Screen Through Colored Cellophane

Investigation Three

I. Objectives of this investigation

The students should be able to:

A. Observe and record the spectra of an electric light bulb, a fluorescent light, and sunlight, using a spectroscope.
B. Compare the spectra of a light bulb, a fluorescent light, and the sun.
C. Observe and record the spectra of the sun, using a prism.
D. Compare the sunlight spectra observed through a spectroscope with that observed through a prism.
E. Infer a reason for the similarities and differences among the spectra of light bulbs, a fluorescent light, and the sun.

II. Materials

A. Spectroscope*: shoe box or round cereal-type box, single-edged razor blade, diffraction grating (2-in. square), double-edged razor blade
B. Clear (unfrosted) light bulb
C. Graph paper (1 sheet)
D. Colored pencils
E. Fluorescent light
F. Prism
G. Textbook
H. Plain white paper

III. Procedure

A. How is the light from an electric light bulb, a fluorescent light and the sun affected by a spectroscope?
   1. Aim the spectroscope (See Appendix 5-1) at the clear (unfrosted) electric light bulb. On a sheet of graph paper, use colored pencils to draw the spectrum you observe.
   2. Aim the spectroscope at a fluorescent light and draw the observed spectrum on the graph paper.
   3. Aim the spectroscope toward the sun, being careful not to look directly at the sun. On the same sheet of graph paper, use colored pencils to draw the spectrum you observe.
   4. Compare the similarities and differences between the spectra of the fluorescent light, an electric light bulb, and the sun.

B. How is the light from the sun affected by passing through a prism?
   1. With your eye almost touching a prism, observe an object in the classroom, such as a textbook standing on the windowsill. The object should be near an electric light or in strong sunlight. If you are holding the prism correctly, several different colors should be seen near the edges of the object. If the colors are not seen, slightly change the position of the prism until you do observe the colors. Record the colors observed.
   2. Move toward the window and allow sunlight to pass through the prism. On the side of the prism away from the window, position a

*See Appendix 5-1: Construction of a Spectroscope.

74

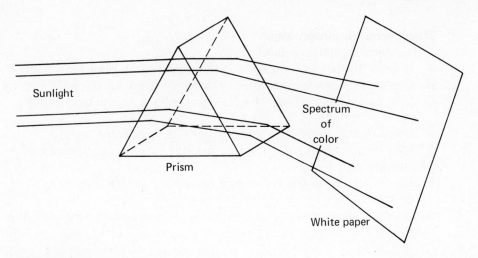

FIGURE 5-5
Light Projected Through a Prism

    piece of paper so that a spectrum of colors falls on the paper. If no
spectrum appears, slightly change the position of the prism until you
observe the colors. (See Figure 5-5.) Record your observations on the
same sheet of graph paper used in step A.

3. Invert the prism from the position it was held in step 2. Compare the
   spectra observed in step 2 with that observed in step 3. In what
   way(s), if any does the position of the prism change the spectrum?

4. Compare the sunlight spectrum observed with a spectroscope with
   that observed with a prism. Record the similarities and differences of
   these spectra.

C. Infer a reason for the similarities and differences among the spectra of
light bulbs, fluorescent light, and the sun.

Investigation Four

I. Objectives of this investigation

The students should be able to:

A. Identify the color produced by different chemicals placed in a flame.

B. Compare the spectra produced by different chemicals placed in a flame.

C. Infer an explanation for the different spectra produced by chemicals placed in a flame.

D. Compare the spectra of a chemical with its flame color.

E. Identify the advantages of using a spectrum for the identification of chemicals.

F. Identify the advantages of using a flame color for the identification of chemicals.

G. Infer the advantages of a spectrum over a flame color for the identification of chemicals.

II. Materials

A. Paper clips (about 10)

B. Paper towel

C. Pliers

D. Chemicals: baking soda, table salt, chalk dust, copper sulfate, barium chloride, calcium nitrate, strontium nitrate, lithium nitrate, and potassium nitrate (small jar of each)

E. Spectroscope (see Investigation Three)

F. Bunsen burner

G. Graph paper

H. Colored pencils

I. Water

III. Procedure

A. What color of light is produced when a chemical is placed in a flame? What type of spectrum is obtained from a chemical placed in a flame?

1. Use a pliers to straighten a paper clip, and to make a small loop at one end of the clip.

2. With the pliers, hold the straight end of the paper clip and place the loop end in the flame of a Bunsen burner. Observe and record the color of the flame. During the remainder of the investigation, this color produced in the flame will indicate there is no chemical left on the paper clip loop.

3. Slightly moisten the loop with water and dip it in baking soda and then hold the loop in the flame. Observe and record the flame color in the table in Figure 5-6. How does this color compare with the color given off by the undipped loop?

4. Again dip the loop in baking soda and observe the flame through your spectroscope. Observe and record on graph paper your observations. Keep the spectroscope close to the flame (about 12 cm away, if possible) but be cautious. You may need a little practice in lining up the slit of the spectroscope with the flame.

Chemical	Flame color
Baking soda	
Chalk dust	
Table salt	
Copper sulfate	
Barium chloride	
Calcium nitrate	
Strontium nitrate	
Lithium nitrate	
Potassium nitrate	

FIGURE 5-6
Table for Identification of Chemical Flame Color

5. Clean the loop by holding it in the flame. Again moisten the loop and dip it in some chalk dust and again hold the loop in the flame. Observe and record, in Figure 5-6, the flame color. Observe the flame through your spectroscope. Record the spectrum on the same graph paper used in step 4.
6. In what way(s), if any, is the spectrum obtained from the burning of baking soda and chalk dust similar to the solar spectrum, the light bulb spectrum, and the fluorescent light spectrum you obtained in Investigation Three?

B. How can a chemical be identified?
1. Using the chemicals in the materials list of this investigation, place a small quantity of one chemical on a clean paper clip loop. Place the loop in the flame. Observe, and record, in Figure 5-6, the flame color.
2. Using the spectroscope, observe and record on the same graph paper used in step A-5, the spectrum of the chemical placed in a flame.
3. Repeat steps 1 and 2, using different chemicals and a clean paper clip loop each time.
4. How does the spectrum of each chemical compare with its flame color?
5. How does the spectra of the different chemicals compare with each other?

C. Identify the advantages of using a flame color for the identification of chemicals.
D. Identify the advantages of using a spectrum for the identification of chemicals.
E. Infer the advantages of a spectrum over a flame color for the identification of chemicals.

Investigation Five

I. Objectives of this investigation
The student should be able to:
A. Measure the distance between two objects, using the method of triangulation.
B. Measure the distance between two objects, using the method of parallax.
C. Infer a method for measuring the distance between the earth and distant objects, such as the moon, sun, and stars.

II. Materials
A. Two straight pins
B. Two soda straws
C. Meterstick
D. Protractor
E. Chalkboard and chalk
F. Metric ruler

III. Procedure
A. How can the distance between two faraway objects be measured?
  1. Put a straight pin all the way through the very middle of each of two soda straws. Stick one pin and soda straw into a meterstick at the 15-cm mark and the other pin and soda straw into the 85-cm mark. The straws should be exactly 70 cm apart. (See Figure 5-7.)
  2. Take the meterstick outside. Place the meterstick on a table, or some other support. Have a classmate stand at one straw and you stand at the other straw. Both of you should close one eye and sight through the straw toward a distant object. When each of you has "focused in" on the object, use a protractor to measure the angle between each soda straw and the meterstick. (See Appendix 2-4: Use of a Protractor.)
  3. You now have three parts of a triangle; a base line (70 cm between the straws) and the two angles just measured. (See Figure 5-8.) Construct a scale drawing of the base line on a piece of paper. If you used a scale of 10 cm to 1 cm, how long would the base line of your scale drawing be? With the protractor, draw the same size angles at the end of the base line that were obtained when the object was sighted

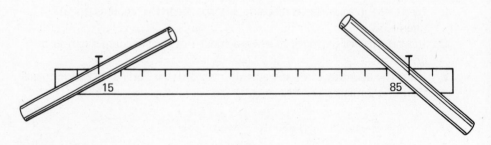

FIGURE 5-7
Meterstick with Soda Straws

78

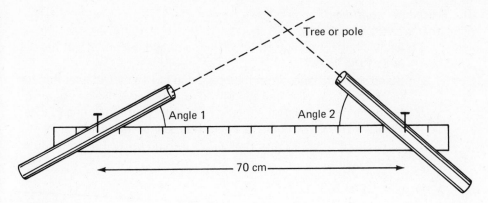

FIGURE 5-8
Three Parts of the Triangle

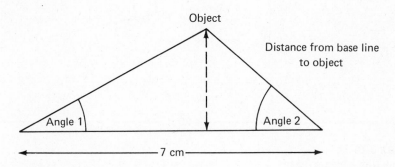

FIGURE 5-9
Scaled Drawing of Observations

through the straws. Extend the sides of the angles until they intersect.

4. Measure the distance from the point where the lines intersect to the base line of your triangle. Using the same scale, how far is it to the faraway object in centimeters? In meters? (See Figure 5-9.)

5. Measure the actual distance to the sighted object. How accurate were you in using this method of indirect measurement (called triangulation)? What factor(s) may have caused inaccuracies in your measurements?

6. Use triangulation to measure the distance to another object that is closer to you. Will the two angles obtained by sighting through the soda straws be larger or smaller than the previous angle measurements? Sight the object and verify your predictions.

7. If the object is a greater distance away from you, what happens to the size of the angles made by the soda straws and the meterstick? What part(s) of the triangulation procedure must be changed in order to measure the distance to an object that is very far away?

8. Using this changed procedure, measure the distance between yourself and an object that is very far away. How accurate were you?

B. How can you more accurately measure the distance between two objects

III. Procedure *(continued)*

that are very far apart?

1. Draw a horizontal line on the chalkboard and put an "X" at the right end of the line.
2. Stand some distance from the board and hold a metric ruler horizontal to the floor, with one end of the ruler placed between your eyes.
3. Hold the other end of the metric ruler with your index finger. (See Figure 5-10.) Close your right eye and use your left eye to sight across your finger toward the "X" at the end of the horizontal line on the board.

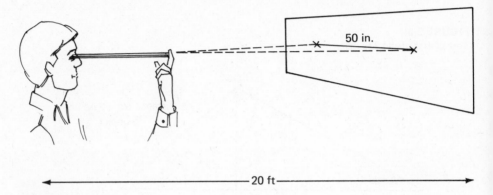

FIGURE 5-10
Sighting with a Metric Ruler

4. Without moving, close your left eye and open your right eye. Have someone mark another "X", according to your direction, on the horizontal line at the point which lines up with your index finger and your right eye. Erase the parts of the line that are not between the two "X's".
5. Measure the distance between your eyes. (This is usually about 6.3 cm.) Measure the length of the line on the chalkboard (in centimeters) and divide this length by 6.3 cm. The result should be the approximate distance in centimeters between you and the chalkboard. Check the accuracy of the distance obtained through the use of your indirect measurement method (called parallax).
6. Move farther away or closer to the chalkboard and repeat the procedure outlined in steps 1 to 4. What differences do you notice in the apparent movement of your index finger each time you vary your distance from the chalkboard? How is the distance from the object you are sighting related to the apparent movement in the position of your index finger?

C. Infer a method for measuring the distance between the earth and a distant object, such as the moon, using the procedures of triangulation and parallax.

Investigation Six

I. Objectives of this investigation

The student should be able to:

A. Observe and record changes in the temperature of equal *volumes* of dry and wet white sand, dry and wet dark sand, and water:
1. Exposed to a heat lamp for five minutes.
2. Allowed to cool for five minutes.

B. Graph the heating and cooling rates for dry and wet white sand, dry and wet dark sand, and water present in equal *volumes.*

C. Compare the rates of heating and cooling for dry and wet white sand, dry and wet dark sand, and water.

D. Predict the temperature at the end of ten minutes for equal *volumes* of dry and wet white sand, dry and wet dark sand, and water exposed to a heat lamp; and again after it has cooled for ten minutes.

E. Verify the predictions concerning the temperature at the end of ten minutes of equal *volumes* of dry and wet white sand, dry and wet dark sand, and water exposed to a heat lamp; and then allowed to cool for ten minutes.

F. Infer an explanation for the observed rates of heating and cooling of equal *volumes* of dry and wet white sand, dry and wet dark sand, and water.

G. Predict the relative heating and cooling rates of equal *weights* of dry and wet white sand, dry and wet dark sand, and water.

H. Verify the prediction concerning the relative heating and cooling rates for equal *weights* of dry and wet white sand, dry and wet dark sand, and water.

I. Graph the heating and cooling rates for dry and wet white sand, dry and wet dark sand, and water present in equal *weights.*

J. Predict the relative heating and cooling rates for *mixtures* of half *dry* white sand and half *dry* dark sand in:
1. Equal volumes.
2. Equal weights.

K. Verify the predictions concerning the relative heating and cooling rates for mixtures of half dry white sand and half dry dark sand in equal volumes; and in equal weights.

L. Predict the relative heating and cooling rates for *mixtures* of half *wet* white sand and half *wet* dark sand in:
1. Equal volumes.
2. Equal weights.

M. Verify the predictions concerning the relative heating and cooling rates for mixtures of half wet white sand and half wet dark sand in equal volumes; and in equal weights.

N. Formulate inferences to explain the heating and cooling rates of the oceans and the land.

II. Materials

A. Graduated cylinder (100 ml)

B. White sand and dark sand (if dark sand is not available, a mixture of

II. **Materials** *(continued)*

   white sand with charcoal powder is satisfactory)
   C. Five test tubes
   D. Five Celsius thermometers
   E. Heat lamp
   F. Laboratory balance
   G. Powdered charcoal (if needed)

III. **Procedure**

   A. How do the heating rates of materials compare?

   1. Carefully measure equal volumes (20 ml) of each of the following substances and put them into separate test tubes. Using the heat lamp, determine the heating rate for each.
       (a) Dry white sand
       (b) Dry dark sand
       (c) Wet white sand
       (d) Wet dark sand
       (e) Water
   2. Observe and record the temperature of each material at one-minute intervals for five minutes. Prepare graphs as shown in Figure 5-11 for each material.
   3. What do you predict will be the temperature of each of the materials at the end of a ten-minute heating period? Verify your predictions.

   B. How do the rates of cooling of the five materials compare?

   1. Determine the rate of cooling for each of the substances.
   2. Construct a graph similar to the one in Figure 5-12 for each material.
   3. How do the temperatures of the five materials compare at the end of the five-minute cooling time?
   4. What do you predict will be the temperature of each material at the

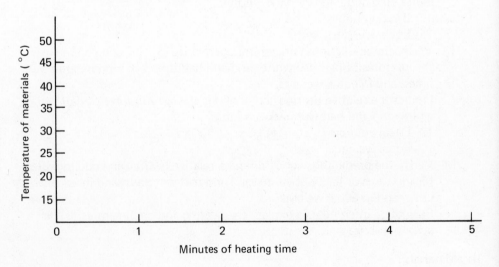

FIGURE 5-11
Graph of Heating Rate

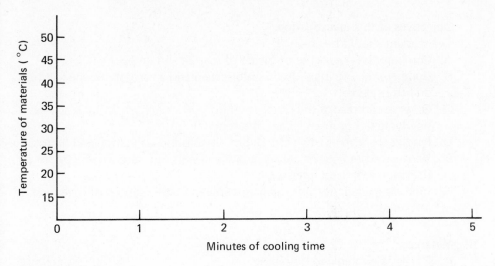

FIGURE 5-12
Graph of Cooling Rate

        end of a ten-minute cooling time? Verify your predictions.

C. What would you predict would be the results if equal **weights** of material were used *instead of equal volumes*?

    1. Determine the heating rates of the materials using equal weights (20 grams) of each material.

    2. Construct the same types of graphs for each material as shown in Figures 5-11 and 5-12.

    3. How do these graphs compare with those constructed in steps A-2 and B-2?

    4. What inferences can you make to explain the observations and comparisons in step 1?

D. What do you predict the heating and cooling rates would be for mixtures of white and dark sand?

    1. Determine the heating and cooling rates for mixtures of dry white sand and dry dark sand, and wet white sand and wet dark sand present in:

        (a) Equal volumes.

        (b) Equal weights.

    2. Prepare graphs of the heating and cooling rates for each of the mixtures.

E. Based on all the observations, comparisons, and graphs that you have made in this investigation, what inferences can you make about the heating and cooling rates for the oceans of the world and the related land areas?

Investigation Seven

I. Objectives of this investigation

The student should be able to:

A. Compare the properties of pieces of marble and limestone.
B. Compare the effects of hydrochloric acid and a carbon dioxide solution on litmus paper.
C. Observe and record the changes that occur when hydrochloric acid is slowly added to marble and limestone.
D. Predict the effects of a carbon dioxide solution on marble and limestone.
E. Verify the predictions concerning the effects of a carbon dioxide solution on marble and limestone.
F. Infer an explanation for the formation and development of caves and related structures.

II. Materials

A. Pieces of marble and limestone
B. Dilute hydrochloric acid—a solution prepared by adding one part of commercially available *concentrated* hydrochloric acid to 12 parts of distilled water. **Use care when using the concentrated hydrochloric acid.**
C. Club soda or seltzer—a carbon dioxide solution (100 ml)
D. Red and blue litmus paper (5 strips each)
E. Medicine dropper

III. Procedure

A. How do the properties of marble and limestone compare?
 1. Observe and list the properties of pieces of marble and limestone.
 2. Identify the similarities and differences between the various rock samples.
B. What is the effect of hydrochloric acid and a carbon dioxide solution on litmus paper?
 1. Determine the effects of both the dilute hydrochloric acid and the carbon dioxide solution on samples of litmus paper.
 2. How do their reactions with litmus paper compare?
C. What is the effect of hydrochloric acid and a carbon dioxide solution on the samples of marble and limestone?
 1. Determine the immediate effects of the liquids on the rock samples.
 2. How do they compare?
 3. What do you predict would happen if the marble and limestone samples were left in the carbon dioxide solution overnight? For a week?
 4. Verify your predictions.
D. Caves and underground caverns are usually formed in rock which has a high concentration of marble and limestone. Infer ways that these structures could have formed and developed in nature.
 1. How could hydrochloric acid be formed in nature?
 2. How could a carbon dioxide solution be formed?

Appendix 1-1: Techniques for Establishing an Aquarium

1. Wash a 1-gal jar with water; do not use soap.
2. Rinse some sand and place it in the bottom of the jar to about a depth of 2 cm.
3. Fill the jar about two-thirds full of water and let it stand for at least 24 hours. (Always have available another container of water that has been allowed to stand at least 24 hours; this water can then be used to replace the water that has evaporated from the aquarium.)
4. After 24 hours, add some water plants to the aquarium, for example, two *Elodea* plants can be dropped into the water and so can some duckweed plants.
5. Drop a few water snails into the aquarium.
6. Put four guppies (two males and two females) into the aquarium.
7. Place the aquarium near a window so that it gets plenty of light, but not direct sunlight.

APPENDIX TWO
Needed Information for Conceptual Scheme II

Appendix 2-1:   Reading a Meterstick

Examine a meterstick and the section of a meterstick pictured in Appendix Figure 2-1. Observe the number and placement of the different length lines in the figure and on the stick. In the figure, long lines appear at the points marked 10 cm (centimeters) and 20 cm. Observe the length of the lines which appear between the 10-cm and the 20-cm marks. The longest lines between these two points are centimeters. One-tenth of a centimeter is a millimeter. How many millimeters are there between the 10-cm and the 11-cm marks? The shortest lines of the meterstick represent millimeters (mm), while the longest lines on most metersticks represent decimeters (dm).

A metric ruler is a portion of the meterstick and is, therefore, read according to the method described here.

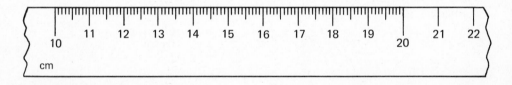

APPENDIX FIGURE 2-1
One Section of a Meterstick

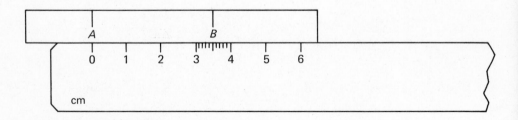

APPENDIX FIGURE 2-2
Distance Between Points *A* and *B*

Appendix 2-2:   Estimating Distances

Examine Appendix Figure 2-2. The distance between lines *A* and *B* is determined by placing the zero point of a metric ruler under line *A* and observing where line *B* falls on the metric ruler. The distance between lines *A* and *B* is greater than 3.0 cm but less than 4.0 cm. Between 3.0 and 4.0 cm there are 10 mm. Estimate how far between 3.5 and 3.6 cm line *B* falls. This number will give you the estimated number of millimeters between lines *A* and *B*. The number is read as 3.54 cm or 35.4 mm.

Appendix 2-3:   Measuring Liquid Volume

Examine the markings on a graduated cylinder. Put some water in the graduated cylinder. Lift the cylinder to eye level. What do you observe about the surface of the water as you look through the cylinder? The liquid level is read at the lowest point of the curved surface. See the liquid level illustrated in Appendix Figure 2-3.

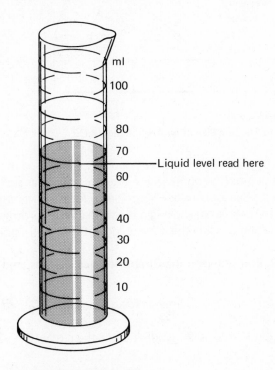

APPENDIX FIGURE 2-3
Level of Liquid in a Graduated Cylinder

Printed near the top of the cylinder is the abbrevialtion "ml" (milliliter). How many milliliters of water can your graduated cylinder contain? How many lines are printed along the side of your cylinder? What is the relationship between this number of lines and the number of milliliters printed near the top of the cylinder?

Appendix 2-4: Use of a Protractor

Observe a protractor: the number of lines from the right edge to the center of the curved edge and from the center to the left edge. Each line represents a unit of measurement, called a degree.

Along the straight edge of the protractor is a line labeled **base line.** The base line is intersected by a line from the 90° mark on the scale. This intersecting line and the base line meet at a 90° angle. The point of intersection is the center of the base line.

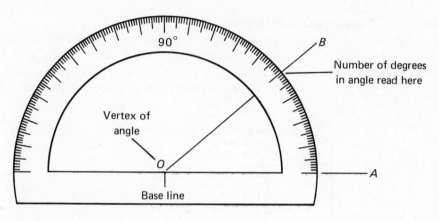

APPENDIX FIGURE 2-4
Protractor Used to Measure Size of an Angle: Angle *AOB*

To measure the degrees in an angle with a protractor, place the midpoint of the base line on the vertex (the point where the sides of the angle meet) of the angle being measured. (See Appendix Figure 2-4 to locate different parts of an angle.) The number of degrees in the angle is read from the protractor at the point where the side of the angle meets the curved edge of the protractor.

Appendix 2-5: Relation Between the Circumference, Radius, and Diameter of a Circle

Circumference of a circle $= \frac{22}{7} \times$ diameter (d) of the circle ($C = \pi d$)

Circumference of a circle $= \frac{22}{7} \times 2 \times$ radius (r) of the circle ($C = \pi 2r$)

Needed Information for APPENDIX
Conceptual Scheme III THREE

Appendix 3-1: Procedure for Preparing Solutions *A* and *B* *

1. Solution *A:*   Slowly add 2.0 grams of *soluble* starch to 500 ml of boiling distilled water. When most of the starch appears to have dissolved, add this to 500 ml of distilled water to make 1 liter of solution. Now, after this solution has cooled, add 0.4 grams of sodium bisulfate. Add 5 ml of a sulfuric acid solution containing 9.8 grams of *concentrated* sulfuric acid in 100 ml of distilled water (add the acid shortly before solution *A* is to be used, as the acid will cause the solution to slowly decompose). The solution can be stored indefinitely if the sulfuric acid is not added until it is to be used.
2. Solution *B:*   Dissolve 2.0 grams of potassium iodate in 1 liter of distilled water. This solution will not decompose and can be stored indefinitely.

Appendix 3-2: Preparation of the Seed Crystals

1. Heat 250 ml of distilled water and slowly add one of the seven compounds, stirring constantly, until little or no more solid will dissolve.
2. Allow the solution to cool and pour the liquid into another beaker. *Save this liquid* as it is the basic growing solution that you will use throughout Investigation Two.
3. Small seed crystals should have formed at the bottom of the original beaker. If they have not, pour the liquid back into this beaker and slowly add more of the compound while you are reheating the solution. After this is done, allow the solution to cool completely and see whether seed crystals have formed.
4. The seed crystals formed can be returned individually to the solution and allowed to grow.

*For ten students.

Appendix 3-3: Preparation of Water Samples and Distillation Apparatus

1. *Preparation of the three water samples*

Sample A	Sample B	Sample C
500 ml distilled water	same	same
37 grams of soil or clay	same	same
50 grams of salt	same	same
4 to 5 drops of food coloring	10 drops of household ammonia	10 drops of vinegar

2. *Preparation of the distillation apparatus*

   Use a 250-ml flask and a one-hole rubber stopper (See Appendix Figure 3-1.)
   Insert a 15-cm piece of glass tubing through the hole so that it extends 5 to 8
   cm into the flask. Attach an 80 to 90 cm piece of rubber tubing to the glass
   tubing. The rubber tubing will lead to a small collecting jar which is placed
   into a large container of iced water.

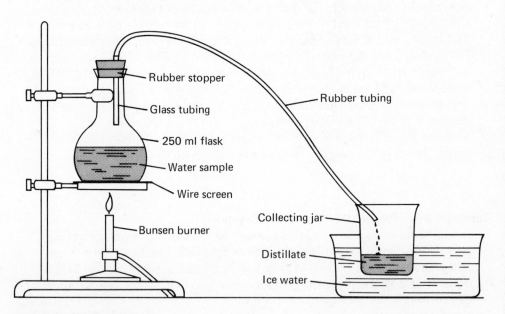

APPENDIX FIGURE 3-1

**Appendix 3-4: Preparation of the Water Samples and Soap and Detergent
Solutions**

1. *Water samples* (for each student):
   (a) Distilled water (500 ml)
   (b) A solution of 20 grams of calcium bicarbonate or magnesium bicarbonate
       in 500 ml of distilled water.
   (c) A solution of 20 grams of calcium chloride or magnesium chloride in 500
       ml of distilled water.

2. *Soap solution* (for 20 students):   This is prepared by allowing one cake of Ivory soap to gradually dissolve in 500 ml of warm water. This should be prepared a day in advance so that the soap will have as much time as possible to dissolve.
3. *Detergent solution* (for 20 students):   This is prepared by slowly dissolving powdered detergent to 500 ml of warm water until no more will dissolve.

Appendix 3-5:   Preparation of Solutions
1. *Acid solutions:*   The acid solutions can be prepared as follows: Dilute commercially available *concentrated* hydrochloric acid and *concentrated* sulfuric acid by slowly adding one part of acid to 20 parts of distilled water. These concentrated acid solutions can be obtained from any commercial chemical supply house.
2. *Phenolphthalein solutions:*   To prepare the red phenolphthalein solution, slowly add sodium hydroxide solution, a drop at a time, to the commercial clear phenolphthalein solution until it turns a pink-red color. If this color slowly fades, add another drop of sodium hydroxide solution until the color is permanent. The original clear phenolphthalein solution can be obtained from any commercial chemical supply house.

Appendix 3-6:   Preparation of the Basic Solutions*
1. Calcium hydroxide: Add 3.7 grams of calcium hydroxide to 1 liter of distilled water.
2. Baking Soda (sodium bicarbonate):   Add 8.4 grams of anhydrous sodium bicarbonate to 1 liter of distilled water.
3. Washing Soda (sodium carbonate):   Add 5.3 grams of anhydrous sodium carbonate to 1 liter of distilled water.
4. Potassium carbonate: Add 13.8 grams of anhydrous potassium carbonate to 1 liter of distilled water.

Appendix 3-7:   Preparation of the Solutions
1. *Acid solutions:*   The hydrochloric acid solution can be prepared by adding one part of commercially available *concentrated* hydrochloric acid to 120 parts of distilled water. The sulfuric acid solution can be prepared by adding one part of commercially available *concentrated* sulfuric acid to 360 parts of distilled water. **Be sure** to add the acid to the water slowly with constant stirring.
2. *Basic solutions* (for 10 students):   The calcium hydroxide solution is prepared by adding 3.7 grams of calcium hydroxide to distilled water to make 1 liter of solution. The sodium hydroxide solution is prepared by adding 4.0 grams of sodium hydroxide to distilled water to make 1 liter of solution. **Care should be taken in handling the sodium hydroxide.**
3. *Sodium chloride solution* (for 10 students):   The sodium chloride solution is prepared by adding 58 grams of sodium chloride to distilled water to make 1 liter of solution.

*For ten students.

Appendix 3-8: Preparation of the Four Solutions

1. This is a chlorophyll extract solution in alcohol. The directions for preparing this solution can be found in Investigation Three, Conceptual Scheme I.

2. A mixture of green and yellow food coloring to match as closely as possible the color of solution number 1. A small amount of alcohol should also be added to make this solution smell like number 1.

3. A solution of potassium permanganate with 1 gram added to 250 ml of water.

4. A mixture of red and blue food coloring to match as closely as possible the color of number 3.

Needed Information for APPENDIX
Conceptual Scheme IV FOUR

Appendix 4-1: Directions for Producing Mold Growth on a Slice of Bread
These directions must be followed about a week before the bread mold is needed.
Moisten a slice of bread (bakery bread is best, since it usually does not contain a
mold inhibitor) with water. Leave the moist bread exposed to the air for several
hours. Then put the bread in a jar and put the lid on, but not too tightly. Keep
the bread damp prior to its use.

**Appendix 4-2: Directions for Transferring Mold from One Slice of Bread to
Another Slice of Bread**
1. Keep the lid on the jar until you are actually transferring the bread mold.
2. A metal instrument, such as a tweezers, is needed for transferring the mold.
   This instrument must be sterilized, which can be done by putting it in the
   flame of a Bunsen burner, candle, or alcohol lamp, until it is red hot. **Caution:
   Use some type of pot holder when you hold the metal instrument in the flame.**
3. Let the instrument cool for several seconds.
4. Using the instrument, remove a small part of the mold from the bread, cover
   the jar, and place the mold on another slice of moist bread.
5. Put the new slice of bread, with the piece of mold on it, into another jar and
   put the lid on, but not too tightly.
6. Sterilize the metal instrument again, even if it is not going to be used.

Appendix 4-3: Preparation of a Euglena Culture
Start your *Euglena* culture three weeks before it is needed. The culturing of
Euglena is very easy. All that is needed is distilled water, plenty of food, and
sunlight.

Clean a glass jar and fill with distilled water. Boil a handful of wheat, rice, or
timothy and add the kernels to the distilled water. Place the jar and its contents
on a windowsill. After a week, add a few drops of concentrated *Euglena. Euglena*
may be purchased from a biological supply house or collected from a stagnant
pool.

In about three weeks, the water should be very green in appearance. Your
culture of *Euglena* is then ready to be used. If additional water is needed, use
distilled water. More food should be added in about two weeks.

Appendix 4-4:   Preparation of Media to Provide the Nourishment for the Bacteria
Either one of the following methods can be used to prepare media to provide
nourishment for the bacteria:

1. Nutrient agar can be purchased from a biological supply house. The directions
    for its preparation will be included with the agar.
2. Obtain a package of unflavored gelatin and follow the directions for its prepa-
    ration. To each cup of the liquid gelatin, add one beef bouillon cube. Boil the
    liquid media for at least ten minutes.

Appendix 4-5:   Preparation of Containers for the Growth of Bacteria
Pour enough of the liquid media into sterilized dishes so that the bottom of each
dish is covered with about a 2-mm layer of media. Sterilized dishes can be obtained in one of the following ways:

1. Presterilized disposable plastic Petri dishes, which can be purchased from a
    biological supply house. These dishes are not reusable.
2. Clean glass Petri dishes (purchased from a biological supply house) can be
    sterilized in an oven at 300° F for at least one hour.

As soon as media is poured into the containers, cover them immediately.
Petri dishes have a top and bottom that fit together, like a pill box. Place the
dishes on a level surface and allow them to gel. These containers can then be
stored in a refrigerator until they are ready to be used.

Appendix 4-6:   Immobilizing Flies
1. Put the flies into a clean, dry jar with a tight fitting lid (such as a baby food
    jar). Place the jar of flies into a container of ice and water. The flies will
    shortly (about eight minutes) collect at the bottom of the jar and will be
    immobilized.
2. In order to examine the flies, they must be kept immobilized without dam-
    aging or killing them. The best method is to keep the flies cool.
3. Completely fill a metal can with crushed ice and water. Dampen a piece of
    nylon mesh (such as a stocking) with ice water and place on the metal can.
    This mesh will prevent the flies from sticking to the metal can and injuring
    them. The flies can then be placed on the cool, mesh-covered can.
4. If the flies become warm, they will begin to move. If this happens, place the
    lid of a Petri dish over the flies and place an ice cube on the Petri dish lid.
    This will cool the trapped air sufficiently to again immobilize the flies. If the
    flies continue to warm up, be sure the metal can is completely filled with
    crushed ice and water. You may have to put some salt into the can with the
    ice-water mixture.
5. After examining the flies, return them to the clean, dry jar until they become
    warm and revive. They can then be transferred to a jar containing media.

Appendix 4-7:   Techniques for Working with Fruit Flies
1. All bottles used in this investigation should first be sterilized by boiling them
    in water for at least twenty minutes.
2. Food (media) for the fruit flies can be obtained from a biological supply

house. Put about 5 cm of media into two sterilized quart milk bottles. Put about 2 cm of media into at least ten small sterilized bottles (such as baby food jars). Close each jar with a sterilized, absorbent cotton plug.

3. When the flies arrive, they will be in small bottles. Transfer the flies from each bottle to their own quart milk bottle (see the following step). Flies will continue to emerge in the small bottles; they should therefore be kept covered. The flies from the small bottles can be continually transferred to the quart milk bottles.

4. Transferring the flies from one bottle to another is an easy task. First hit the bottom of the two jars with your hand; this will knock the flies off the cotton plugs. Quickly remove the cotton plug and hold the "mouths" of the two jars together (the jar the flies are to be transferred from should be on the bottom). Cover the bottom jar with dark paper and the flies will move toward the light (the top jar). Separate the two jars and quickly put the cotton plugs back in their "mouths."

5. Male and female flies can easily be distinguished. Use a hand lens to examine the abdomen of the flies. The female has a broader abdomen than the male. The female has small lines across her abdomen, while the male has a black-tipped abdomen.

6. In order to have accurate results, only virgin females can be used in mating. Remove some of the pupae from your quart bottles and place them in clean small bottles (without media), and plug with cotton. As soon as the flies emerge, immobilize them by cooling. Place three virgin females and three males in a small bottle containing about 2 cm of media. Be careful not to place the immobilized flies directly on the media, as they will stick to it. Record the date, your name, and the type of flies being mated on a piece of paper and attach it to the jar. Ten days later, remove the original flies so they will not be included in your results. As soon as the offspring flies emerge, count them each day for ten days. After the flies have been counted, they can be released outside the building.

APPENDIX FIVE
Needed Information for Conceptual Scheme V

Appendix 5-1: Construction of a Spectroscope

In the center of one end of the box, cut a vertical slit 1 in. long. This slit should be as narrow and straight-edged as possible. A double-edged razor blade broken in half and placed on each side of the slit will enable you to make a straight slit and one whose width can be easily adjusted.

In the center of the other end of the box, cut a hole 1 in. square. Hold a piece of diffraction grating over this hole. Put the cover on the shoe box and aim the slit in the end of the box toward a source of light. Look through the grating. You should see two horizontal spectra, one on each side of the slit. If the spectra are not horizontal, rotate the piece of diffraction grating until they become horizontal. Now tape the diffraction grating in place over the 1-in.-square hole.

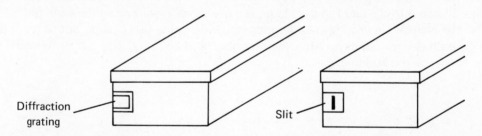

Diffraction grating

Slit

APPENDIX FIGURE 5-1
Ends of the Shoe Box

96

Conceptual Scheme I: Matter and Energy Interact Between Living Organisms and Their Environment

1. Grow plants in red, green, and blue light, sunlight, and darkness.
2. Compare the characteristics of plants grown in red, green, and blue light, sunlight, and darkness.
3. Formulate hypotheses regarding the differences in the characteristics of plants grown in red, green, and blue light, sunlight, and darkness.
4. Isolate the variables that affect the characteristics of plants grown in red, green, and blue light, sunlight, and darkness.
5. Plan and conduct an experiment to explain the differences in the characteristics of plants grown in red, green, and blue light, sunlight, and darkness.
6. Make predictions regarding the characteristics of plants grown in red-green, red-blue, and blue-green light.
7. Verify the predictions regarding the characteristics of plants grown in red-green, red-blue, and blue-green light.
8. Infer an explanation for the characteristics of trees growing in a dense forest.
9. Identify the direction that plants grow in relation to a light source.
10. Infer an explanation for the direction that plants grow in relation to a light source.
11. Compare the heights of plants grown under varying proportions of light and dark.
12. Graph the height of a plant against the number of hours of light per 24 hours that the plant received.
13. Infer an explanation for the different heights of plants grown under varying proportions of light and dark.
14. Infer a relationship between the direction plants grow and the proportion of light they receive.
15. Verify the presence of starch in the leaves of plants.
16. Isolate the variables that will affect the production of starch in plants.
17. Plan and conduct an experiment to determine those variables which will affect the production of starch in plants.
18. Verify the presence of carbon dioxide in your breath.
19. Formulate an hypothesis to explain why a bromthymol blue solution changes

Conceptual Scheme I *(continued)*

       color when a plant is placed in the solution.

20. Isolate the variables that will affect a plant's reaction to a bromthymol blue solution.
21. Plan and conduct an experiment to determine which variables will affect a plant's reaction to a bromthymol blue solution.
22. Infer a relationship between starch production in a plant and the plant's reaction to a bromthymol blue solution.
23. Compare a system containing a phenol red solution and a plant with a system containing a phenol red solution and an animal, both systems having been kept in the light for 24 hours.
24. Infer an explanation for the similarities and differences in two systems (plant and phenol red solution; animal and phenol red solution) that have been kept in the light for 24 hours.
25. Make predictions regarding the effect of plants and animals on phenol red solutions after the systems have been in the dark for 24 hours.
26. Verify the predictions regarding the effect of plants and animals on phenol red solutions after the systems have been in the dark for 24 hours.
27. Compare the effects of plants and animals on phenol red solutions placed in the light for 24 hours and in the dark for 24 hours.
28. Infer an explanation for the comparison of phenol red solutions placed in the light for 24 hours and in the dark for 24 hours, one system containing plants and the other system containing animals.
29. Compare lima beans, raisins, and prunes soaked in water with those not soaked in water.
30. Make inferences to explain the differences among soaked and unsoaked lima beans, raisins, and prunes.
31. Compare the changes that take place in and around three pieces of dialysis tubing soaked in water: one piece containing sugar and water; one piece containing corn syrup; and the third piece containing water.
32. Formulate an hypothesis to explain the changes that occur in and around three pieces of dialysis tubing soaked in water: one piece containing sugar and water; one piece containing corn syrup; and the third piece containing water.
33. Plan and conduct an experiment to explain the changes that occur in and around three pieces of dialysis tubing soaked in water: one piece containing sugar and water; one piece containing corn syrup; and the third piece containing water.
34. Predict the similarities of plastic wrap, wax paper, and cellophane with dialysis tubing.
35. Verify the predictions of the similarities of plastic wrap, wax paper, and cellophane with dialysis tubing.
36. Infer an explanation for the passage of water into a plant.
37. Observe and list the characteristics of mealworms.
38. Formulate hypotheses concerning the abilities of mealworms to see, hear, and smell.

39. Plan and conduct experiments to test the hypotheses concerning the ability of mealworms to see, hear, and smell.
40. Formulate hypotheses concerning the foods that the mealworms prefer to eat.
41. Plan and conduct experiments to test the hypotheses concerning the foods that mealworms prefer to eat.
42. Set up an aquarium.
43. Observe and list the changes that occur in an aquarium over an extended period of time.
44. Formulate an hypothesis to explain the changes that occur in an aquarium.
45. Isolate the variables involved in tests regarding changes in an aquarium.
46. Plan and conduct an experiment to investigate the causes of changes in an aquarium.
47. Infer a relationship of plants and animals in an aquarium.

Conceptual Scheme II: Matter Can Be Measured in Mathematical Units and These Units Exist in Orderly Systems

1. Measure the distance between markings in this book, in metric units.
2. Measure the volume of a solid and of a liquid, in metric units.
3. Compare the change in the volume of water in a container with the volume of a solid object when it is submerged in the water.
4. Identify a procedure to measure, in metric units, the volume of an irregular shaped object.
5. Measure the weight of an object in metric units.
6. Predict the weight of a metal block in air, cooking oil, vinegar, and motor oil.
7. Verify the predictions concerning the weight of a metal block in air, cooking oil, vinegar, and motor oil.
8. Compare the weight in water of a metal, wooden, plastic, and aluminum foil block.
9. Isolate the variables which affect the weight of different blocks of materials placed in several different liquids.
10. Plan and conduct an experiment to determine which variables affect the weight of different blocks of materials placed in several different liquids.
11. Predict the results of placing a sheet of aluminum foil and a ball of aluminum foil on the surface of a liquid.
12. Verify the predictions concerning the results of placing a sheet of aluminum foil and a ball of aluminum foil on the surface of a liquid.
13. Infer an explanation as to why boats float.
14. Compare the weight of equal volumes of water, alcohol, olive oil, pentane, and turpentine.
15. Infer why all liquids do or do not have the same weight.
16. Compare the weight/volume ratio of water with the weight/volume ratio of alcohol, olive oil, pentane, and turpentine.
17. Predict whether ice will float on alcohol, olive oil, pentane, and turpentine.
18. Verify the predictions concerning whether ice will float on alcohol, olive oil, pentane, and turpentine.
19. Measure temperature, in both Fahrenheit and Celsius units.
20. Hypothesize reasons for the different temperature readings recorded throughout the classroom.
21. Predict the temperature, in both Fahrenheit and Celsius units, of various locations outside the classroom.
22. Verify the predictions concerning the temperature of various locations outside the classroom.
23. Measure the size of an angle, a circle, and a sphere, using a protractor.
24. Rank four angles in order from largest to smallest.
25. Identify the dimensions of a sphere that must be changed in order to alter the size of the whole sphere.
26. Measure time without using a clock or watch.

Conceptual Scheme III: Changes in Matter Require Energy and the Totality of Matter and Energy Is Conserved

1. Predict the rate of a chemical reaction when:
    (a) Particle size is changed.
    (b) Concentration is changed.
    (c) Surface area is changed.
    (d) Temperature is changed.
2. Verify the predictions concerning the rate of a chemical reaction when:
    (a) Particle size is changed.
    (b) Concentration is changed.
    (c) Surface area is changed.
    (d) Temperature is changed.
3. Make inferences concerning the nature of chemical reactions.
4. Prepare and grow crystals of at least one of the following compounds:
    (a) Potassium dichromate
    (b) Cupric sulfate
    (c) Nickelous sulfate
    (d) Potassium sulfate
    (e) Sodium chloride
    (f) Potassium aluminum sulfate (alum)
    (g) Potassium chromium sulfate (chrome alum)
5. Predict the effect on the growth of a crystal by changing the rate of evaporation of the growing solution.
6. Plan and conduct an experiment to determine the effect on the growth of a crystal by changing the rate of evaporation of the growing solution.
7. Graph the rate of growth of the seed crystals.
8. Predict the size of one crystal after one month's growth.
9. Compare the properties of all the crystals produced and grown by the other members of the class.
10. Predict which compound would produce the largest crystal at the end of a specified period of time.
11. Predict the effects on the growth of a crystal by:
    (a) Adding a second compound to the growing solution.
    (b) Breaking the seed crystal.
12. Plan and conduct an experiment to determine the effects on the growth of a crystal by:
    (a) Adding a second compound to the growing solution.
    (b) Breaking the seed crystal.
13. Infer factors that might affect the growth of a crystal.
14. Compare the properties of three water samples before and after:
    (a) Boiling for five minutes.
    (b) Filtering through filter paper.
    (c) Filtering through filter paper and activated charcoal.
    (d) Distillation.
15. Identify a procedure to remove the greatest number of impurities from a water sample.

Conceptual Scheme III *(continued)*

16. Plan and conduct an experiment, using the identified procedure, to purify a water sample.
17. Infer the properties of water samples found:
    (a) At the base of a waterfall.
    (b) In a polluted river.
    (c) In the ocean.
    (d) In a stagnant lake.
    (e) In a fast flowing mountain stream.
18. Observe and list the properties of three water samples before and after boiling; and after filtering.
19. Identify a procedure to determine the sudsing ability of three water samples.
20. Compare the ability of three water samples to form suds.
21. Compare the effects on the sudsing ability of water samples of boiling; and filtering.
22. Identify a procedure to determine the purity of a water sample.
23. Plan and conduct an experiment, using the identified procedure to determine the purity of a water sample.
24. Compare the properties of different acid solutions.
25. Compare the effects of different acid solutions on pieces of litmus paper, and on solutions of phenolphthalein, congo red, red cabbage juice, and grape juice.
26. Compare the effects of different acid solutions on pieces of zinc, marble, and aluminum.
27. Identify a procedure to determine whether a substance is an acid.
28. Plan and conduct an experiment, using the identified procedure, to determine whether a substance is an acid.
29. Identify a procedure to determine which of two acids is the stronger.
30. Plan and conduct an experiment, using the identified procedure, to determine which of the two acids is the stronger.
31. Compare the properties of different basic solutions.
32. Compare the effects of different basic solutions on pieces of litmus paper and solutions of phenolphthalein, congo red, red cabbage juice, and grape juice.
33. Compare the effects of different basic solutions on pieces of marble, aluminum, and samples of grease.
34. Identify a procedure to determine whether a substance is basic.
35. Plan and conduct an experiment, using the identified procedure, to determine whether an unknown substance is basic.
36. Identify a procedure to determine which of two basic solutions is the stronger.
37. Plan and conduct an experiment, using the identified procedure, to determine which of two basic solutions is the stronger.
38. Observe and list the properties of liquids formed by mixing together solutions of acids and bases.
39. Predict the effects of neutralized acid and base solutions on litmus paper, and solutions of phenolphthalein, congo red, red cabbage juice, and grape juice.

40. Verify the predictions concerning the effects of neutralized acid and base solutions on litmus paper, and solutions of phenolphthalein, congo red, red cabbage juice, and grape juice.
41. Predict the effects of neutralized acid and base solutions on pieces of marble, zinc, and aluminum.
42. Verify the predictions concerning the effects of neutralized acid and base solutions on pieces of marble, zinc, and aluminum.
43. Identify a procedure to determine whether a solution is neutral, that is, neither an acid nor a base.
44. Plan and conduct an experiment, using the identified procedure, to determine if a solution is neutral.
45. Compare the changes that occur in identical strips of paper which are placed in several different solutions.
46. Compare the effects of several different types of paper placed in the same solution.
47. Identify the number of ingredients in an unknown solution.
48. Identify an unknown solution.
49. Predict changes that would occur in identical strips of paper placed in a mixture of several different solutions.
50. Plan and conduct an experiment to verify the prediction concerning the changes that would occur in identical strips of paper placed in a mixture of several different solutions.
51. Observe and list the characteristics of a moving pendulum.
52. Identify one or more methods for determining the rate of motion of a pendulum.
53. Isolate the variables that might affect the rate of motion of a pendulum.
54. Hypothesize the variables that would affect the rate of motion of a pendulum.
55. Plan and conduct an experiment to test the hypothesis concerning the variables which affect the rate of motion of a pendulum.
56. Identify the materials which are, and are not, attracted by a magnet.
57. Classify materials attracted by a magnet according to their physical properties.
58. Identify the direction a freely turning bar magnet will point when it stops turning.
59. Identify the direction compass needles will point when placed in an open area.
60. Compare the behavior of a suspended bar magnet with the behavior of a compass needle.
61. Hypothesize the relationship(s) between the behavior of a compass needle and that of a bar magnet.
62. Identify the poles of an unmarked magnet.
63. Observe and record what happens to iron filings sprinkled on a piece of paper which is placed on top of a magnet.
64. Make inferences to explain observations of iron filings sprinkled on a piece of paper which is placed on top of a magnet.
65. Infer an explanation for the direction(s) a compass needle points when it is placed in various positions around the magnet.

Conceptual Scheme III *(continued)*

66. Observe and record what happens to iron filings sprinkled on a piece of paper that has a current-carrying wire projecting through the center.

67. Make inferences to explain observations of iron filings placed on a piece of paper that has a current-carrying wire projecting through the center.

68. Predict the direction(s) a compass needle will point when brought close to a wire carrying an electric current.

69. Verify the predictions concerning the direction(s) a compass needle will point when brought close to a wire carrying an electric current.

70. Make inferences to explain the direction(s) a compass needle will point when brought close to a wire carrying an electric current.

71. Predict the position(s) of (1) iron filings and (2) a compass needle placed on a piece of paper over (1) a single loop of wire carrying an electric current and (2) a coil of wire carrying an electric current.

72. Verify the predictions concerning the position(s) of (1) iron filings and (2) a compass needle placed on a piece of paper over (1) a single loop of wire carrying an electric current and (2) a coil of wire carrying an electric current.

73. Make inferences to explain the position(s) of (1) iron filings and (2) a compass needle placed on a piece of paper over (1) a single loop of wire carrying an electric current and (2) a coil of wire carrying an electric current.

74. Predict the way(s) one flashlight bulb, one wire, and a dry cell can be connected so that the bulb will light.

75. Verify the predictions concerning the way(s) one flashlight bulb, one wire, and one dry cell can be connected so that the bulb will light.

76. Infer the path taken by electricity to light a flashlight bulb when one wire and a dry cell are used.

77. Predict the way(s) one flashlight bulb and holder, two wires, and a dry cell can be connected so that the bulb will light.

78. Verify the predictions concerning the way(s) one flashlight bulb and holder, two wires, and a dry cell can be connected so that the bulb will light.

79. Infer the path taken by electricity to light a flashlight bulb when two wires and one dry cell are used.

80. Predict the way(s) two flashlight bulbs, two wires, and a dry cell can be connected so that the bulbs will light.

81. Verify the predictions concerning the way(s) two flashlight bulbs, two wires, and a dry cell can be connected so that the bulb will light.

82. Predict the way(s) one end of a wire can be disconnected causing one and then two flashlight bulbs to go out.

83. Verify the predictions concerning the way(s) one end of a wire can be disconnected so that one and then two flashlight bulbs will go out.

84. Predict the way(s) two flashlight bulbs, three wires, and a dry cell can be connected so that the bulbs will light.

85. Verify the predictions concerning the way(s) two flashlight bulbs, three wires, and a dry cell can be connected so that the bulbs will light.

86. Predict the way(s) two flashlight bulbs, four wires, and a dry cell can be connected so that the bulbs will light.

87. Verify the predictions concerning the way(s) two flashlight bulbs, four wires, and a dry cell can be connected so that the bulbs will light.
88. Compare the properties of two lighted flashlight bulbs when they are both connected to a dry cell by two, three, and four wires.
89. Hypothesize a cause for inconsistent results among classmates concerning the observed properties of two lighted flashlight bulbs.
90. Isolate the variables which caused inconsistencies among the class concerning the observed properties of two lighted bulbs.
91. Plan and conduct an experiment to determine the cause of inconsistent results among the class concerning the observed properties of two lighted bulbs.
92. Infer an explanation for the properties of two lighted flashlight bulbs connected to a dry cell by two, three, and four wires.

Conceptual Scheme IV: Living Organisms Are a Product of Heredity and Environment

1.   Compare the characteristics of seeds.
2.   Compare the germination times of seeds.
3.   Identify the location(s) of growth in the leaf and stem of a plant.
4.   Predict the location(s) of growth in the root of a plant.
5.   Verify the prediction of the location(s) of growth in the root of a plant.
6.   Infer the location(s) of growth in a tree.
7.   Observe and list the characteristics of mold on bread.
8.   Isolate the variables that will affect the growth of mold on bread.
9.   Identify a procedure to measure the amount of mold growth on bread.
10.   Plan and conduct an experiment to determine which variables will affect the growth of mold on bread.
11.   Observe and describe the various structures of a flower.
12.   Infer from observations of a flower, a function for each of its structures.
13.   Compare albino corn seeds.
14.   Predict the characteristics of the plants that will germinate from corn seeds.
15.   Verify the predictions of the characteristics of the plants that will germinate from corn seeds.
16.   Make inferences regarding the causes for the characteristics of corn plants.
17.   Observe and draw the component parts (cells) of different living organisms, using a microscope.
18.   Compare the cells from the same and from different living organisms.
19.   Prepare a *Euglena* culture.
20.   Observe and draw *Euglena,* using a microscope.
21.   Identify a procedure to measure the size of an individual *Euglena*.
22.   Observe and describe the method of reproduction used by *Euglena*.
23.   Identify a procedure to measure the rate of reproduction for *Euglena*.
24.   Isolate the variables that affect the behavior of *Euglena*.
25.   Plan and conduct an experiment to determine which variables affect the behavior of *Euglena*.
26.   Observe and list the characteristics of a colony of bacteria.
27.   Infer an explanation for the number of colonies of bacteria growing on an inoculated Petri dish.
28.   Compare the number of colonies of bacteria growing on Petri dishes inoculated with various materials.
29.   Infer an explanation for the differences in the number of colonies of bacteria on Petri dishes inoculated with various materials.
30.   Hypothesize methods of inhibiting the growth of bacteria.
31.   Plan and conduct an experiment to determine: (1) environmental conditions that will inhibit the growth of bacteria and (2) chemical substances that will inhibit the growth of bacteria.
32.   Infer methods of preventing an infection caused by bacteria.
33.   Classify all the students in the classroom who can, and cannot, taste the chemical on a piece of PTC paper.
34.   Formulate an hypothesis to explain why some students can, and other students cannot, taste the chemical on a piece of PTC paper.

35. Plan and conduct an experiment regarding the ability of some students to taste the chemical on a piece of PTC paper.
36. Make predictions regarding the ability of other people to taste the chemical on a piece of PTC paper.
37. Compare the characteristics of fruit flies *(Drosophila)*.
38. Formulate an hypothesis to explain the characteristics of the offspring resulting from the mating of selected fruit flies.
39. Plan and conduct an experiment to determine the characteristics of the offspring resulting from the mating of selected fruit flies.
40. Infer an explanation for the similarities and differences of children with their parents.

Conceptual Scheme V: The Physical Universe, and All Systems in It, Are Constantly Changing

1. Identify the direction(s) light travels from a light bulb.
2. Infer the direction of travel of a beam of light from a bulb.
3. Graph the area lighted by a bulb against the distance between the bulb and that area.
4. Use a graph to predict the area lighted when a bulb is placed at different distances from that area.
5. Verify the predictions of the area lighted when a bulb is placed at different distances from that area.
6. Identify the color projected on a screen when pieces of cellophane are placed between a light source and the screen.
7. Predict the color that will be projected on a screen when the screen and the cellophane are the same color.
8. Verify the predictions concerning the color projected on the screen when the screen and the cellophane are the same color.
9. Predict the color to be projected on a screen when the screen and the cellophane are different colors (the screen not being white).
10. Verify the predictions concerning the color projected on a screen when the screen and the cellophane are different colors (the screen not being white).
11. Formulate inferences to explain why objects appear to be of different colors.
12. Observe and record the spectra of an electric light bulb, a fluorescent light, and sunlight, using a spectroscope.
13. Compare the spectra of a light bulb, a fluorescent light, and the sun.
14. Observe and record the spectra of the sun, using a prism.
15. Compare the sunlight spectra observed through a spectroscope with that observed through a prism.
16. Infer a reason for the similarities and differences among the spectra of light bulbs, a fluorescent light, and the sun.
17. Identify the color produced by different chemicals placed in a flame.
18. Compare the spectra produced by different chemicals placed in a flame.
19. Infer an explanation for the different spectra produced by chemicals placed in a flame.
20. Compare the spectra of a chemical with its flame color.
21. Identify the advantages of using a spectrum for the identification of chemicals.
22. Identify the advantages of using a flame color for the identification of chemicals.
23. Infer the advantages of a spectrum over a flame color for the identification of chemicals.
24. Measure the distance between two objects, using the method of triangulation.
25. Measure the distance between two objects, using the method of parallax.
26. Infer a method for measuring the distance between the earth and distant objects, such as the moon, sun, and stars.
27. Observe and record changes in the temperature of equal *volumes* of dry and wet white sand, dry and wet dark sand, and water:
    (a) Exposed to a heat lamp for five minutes.
    (b) Allowed to cool for five minutes.

28. Graph the heating and cooling rates for dry and wet white sand, dry and wet dark sand, and water present in equal *volumes.*

29. Compare the rates of heating and cooling for dry and wet white sand, dry and wet dark sand, and water.

30. Predict the temperature at the end of ten minutes for equal *volumes* of dry and wet white sand, dry and wet dark sand, and water exposed to a heat lamp; and again after it has cooled for ten minutes.

31. Verify the predictions concerning the temperature at the end of ten minutes of equal *volumes* of dry and wet white sand, dry and wet dark sand, and water exposed to a heat lamp; and then allowed to cool for ten minutes.

32. Infer an explanation for the observed rates of heating and cooling of equal *volumes* of dry and wet white sand, dry and wet dark sand, and water.

33. Predict the relative heating and cooling rates of equal *weights* of dry and wet white sand, dry and wet dark sand, and water.

34. Verify the prediction concerning the relative heating and cooling rates for equal *weights* of dry and wet white sand, dry and wet dark sand, and water.

35. Graph the heating and cooling rates for dry and wet white sand, dry and wet dark sand, and water present in equal *weights.*

36. Predict the relative heating and cooling rates for *mixtures* of half *dry* white sand and half *dry* dark sand in:
    (a)   Equal volumes.
    (b)   Equal weights.

37. Verify the predictions concerning the relative heating and cooling rates for mixtures of half dry white sand and half dry dark sand in equal volumes; and in equal weights.

38. Predict the relative heating and cooling rates for *mixtures* of half *wet* white sand and half *wet* dark sand in:
    (a)   Equal volumes.
    (b)   Equal weights.

39. Verify the predictions concerning the relative heating and cooling rates for mixtures of half wet white sand and half wet dark sand in equal volumes; and in equal weights.

40. Formulate inferences to explain the heating and cooling rates of the oceans and the land.

41. Compare the properties of pieces of marble and limestone.

42. Compare the effects of hydrochloric acid and a carbon dioxide solution on litmus paper.

43. Observe and record the changes that occur when hydrochloric acid is slowly added to marble and limestone.

44. Predict the effects of a carbon dioxide solution on marble and limestone.

45. Verify the predictions concerning the effects of a carbon dioxide solution on marble and limestone.

46. Infer an explanation for the formation and development of caves and related structures.

APPENDIX Objectives by
SEVEN Skills

I. Psychomotor Skills
1. Grow plants in red, green, and blue light, sunlight, and darkness.
2. Set up an aquarium.
3. Measure the distance between markings in this book, in metric units.
4. Measure the volume of a solid and of a liquid, in metric units.
5. Measure the weight of an object, in metric units.
6. Measure temperature, in both Fahrenheit and Celsius units.
7. Measure the size of an angle, a circle, and a sphere, using a protractor.
8. Prepare and grow crystals of at least one of the following compounds:
    (a) Potassium dichromate
    (b) Cupric sulfate
    (c) Nickelous sulfate
    (d) Potassium sulfate
    (e) Sodium chloride
    (f) Potassium aluminum sulfate (alum)
    (g) Potassium chromium sulfate (chrome alum)
9. Prepare a *Euglena* culture.

II. Inquiry Skills
A. Observation
1. Observe and list the characteristics of mealworms.
2. Observe and list the changes that occur in an aquarium over an extended period of time.
3. Observe and list the properties of three water samples before and after boiling; and after filtering.
4. Observe and list the properties of liquids formed by mixing together solutions of acids and bases.
5. Observe and list the characteristics of a moving pendulum.
6. Observe and record what happens to iron filings sprinkled on a piece of paper that is placed on top of a magnet.
7. Observe and record what happens to iron filings sprinkled on a piece of paper that has a current-carrying wire projecting through the center.

8. Observe and list the characteristics of mold on bread.
9. Observe and describe the various structures of a flower.
10. Observe and draw the component parts (cells) of different living organisms, using a microscope.
11. Observe and draw *Euglena,* using a microscope.
12. Observe and describe the method of reproduction used by *Euglena.*
13. Observe and list the characteristics of a colony of bacteria.
14. Observe and record the spectra of an electric light bulb, a fluorescent light, and sunlight, using a spectroscope.
15. Observe and record the spectra of the sun, using a prism.
16. Observe and record changes in the temperature of equal *volumes* of dry and wet white sand, dry and wet dark sand, and water:
    (a) Exposed to a heat lamp for five minutes.
    (b) Allowed to cool for five minutes.
17. Observe and record the changes that occur when hydrochloric acid is slowly added to marble and limestone.

B. Comparison

1. Compare the characteristics of plants grown in red, green, and blue light, sunlight, and darkness.
2. Compare the heights of plants grown under varying proportions of light and dark.
3. Compare a system containing a phenol red solution and a plant with a system containing a phenol red solution and an animal, both systems having been kept in the light for 24 hours.
4. Compare the effects of plants and animals on phenol red solutions placed in the light for 24 hours and in the dark for 24 hours.
5. Compare lima beans, raisins, and prunes soaked in water with those not soaked in water.
6. Compare the changes that take place in and around three pieces of dialysis tubing soaked in water: one piece containing sugar and water; one piece containing corn syrup; and the third piece containing water.
7. Compare the change in the volume of water in a container with the volume of a solid object when it is submerged in the water.
8. Compare the weight in water of a metal, wooden, plastic, and aluminum foil block.
9. Compare the weight of equal volumes of water, alcohol, olive oil, pentane, and turpentine.
10. Compare the weight/volume ratio of water with the weight/volume ratio of alcohol, olive oil, pentane, and turpentine.
11. Compare the properties of all the crystals produced and grown by the other members of the class.
12. Compare the ability of three water samples to form suds.
13. Compare the effects on the sudsing ability of water samples of boiling; and filtering.
14. Compare the properties of three water samples before and after:
    (a) Boiling for five minutes.

B. Comparison *(continued)*

      (b)   Filtering through filter paper.

     ·(c)   Filtering through filter paper and activated charcoal.

      (d)   Distillation.

15. Compare the properties of different acid solutions.

16. Compare the effects of different acid solutions on pieces of litmus paper, and on solutions of phenolphthalein, congo red, red cabbage juice, and grape juice.

17. Compare the effects of different acid solutions on pieces of zinc, marble, and aluminum.

18. Compare the properties of different basic solutions.

19. Compare the effects of different basic solutions on pieces of litmus paper, and on solutions of phenolphthalein, congo red, red cabbage juice, and grape juice.

20. Compare the effects of different basic solutions on pieces of marble, aluminum, and samples of grease.

21. Compare the changes that occur in identical strips of paper which are placed in several different solutions.

22. Compare the effects of several different types of paper placed in the same solution.

23. Compare the behavior of a suspended bar magnet with the behavior of a compass needle.

24. Compare the properties of two lighted flashlight bulbs when they are both connected to a dry cell by two, three, and four wires.

25. Compare the characteristics of seeds.

26. Compare the germination times of seeds.

27. Compare albino corn seeds.

28. Compare the cells from the same and from different living organisms.

29. Compare the number of colonies of bacteria growing on Petri dishes inoculated with various materials.

30. Compare the characteristics of fruit flies *(Drosophila).*

31. Compare the sunlight spectra observed through a spectroscope with that observed through a prism.

32. Compare the spectra of a light bulb, a fluorescent light, and the sun.

33. Compare the spectra produced by different chemicals placed in a flame.

34. Compare the spectra of a chemical with its flame color.

35. Compare the rates of heating and cooling for dry and wet white sand, dry and wet dark sand, and water.

36. Compare the properties of pieces of marble and limestone.

37. Compare the effects of hydrochloric acid and a carbon dioxide solution on litmus paper.

C. Identification

1. Identify the direction that plants grow in relation to a light source.

2. Identify a procedure to measure, in metric units, the volume of an irregular shaped object.

3. Identify the dimensions of a sphere that must be changed in order to alter the size of the whole sphere.
4. Identify a procedure to determine the sudsing ability of three water samples.
5. Identify a procedure to determine the purity of a water sample.
6. Identify a procedure to remove the greatest number of impurities from a water sample.
7. Identify a procedure to determine whether a substance is an acid.
8. Identify a procedure to determine which of two acids is the stronger.
9. Identify a procedure to determine whether a substance is basic.
10. Identify a procedure to determine which of two basic solutions is the stronger.
11. Identify a procedure to determine whether a solution is neutral, that is, neither an acid nor a base.
12. Identify the number of ingredients in an unknown solution.
13. Identify an unknown solution.
14. Identify one or more methods for determining the rate of motion of a pendulum.
15. Identify the materials that are, and are not, attracted by a magnet.
16. Identify the direction a freely turning bar magnet will point when it stops turning.
17. Identify the direction compass needles will point when placed in an open area.
18. Identify the poles of an unmarked magnet.
19. Identify the location(s) of growth in the leaf and stem of a plant.
20. Identify a procedure to measure the amount of mold growth on bread.
21. Identify a procedure to measure the size of an individual *Euglena*.
22. Identify a procedure to measure the rate of reproduction for *Euglena*.
23. Identify the direction(s) light travels from a light bulb.
24. Identify the color projected on a screen when pieces of cellophane are placed between a light source and the screen.
25. Identify the color produced by different chemicals placed in a flame.
26. Identify the advantages of using a spectrum for the identification of chemicals.
27. Identify the advantages of using a flame color for the identification of chemicals.

D. Classification

1. Graph the height of a plant against the number of hours of light per 24 hours that the plant received.
2. Graph the rate of growth of the seed crystals.
3. Classify materials attracted by a magnet according to their physical properties.
4. Classify all the students in the classroom who can, and cannot, taste the chemical on a piece of PTC paper.
5. Graph the area lighted by a bulb against the distance between the

D. **Classification** *(continued)*
bulb and that area.
6. Graph the heating and cooling rates for dry and wet white sand, dry and wet dark sand, and water present in equal *volumes.*
7. Graph the heating and cooling rates for dry and wet white sand, dry and wet dark sand, and water present in equal *weights.*

E. **Measurement**
1. Measure time without using a clock or watch.
2. Measure the distance between two objects, using the method of triangulation.
3. Measure the distance between two objects, using the method of parallax.

F. **Inference**
1. Infer an explanation for the characteristics of trees growing in a dense forest.
2. Infer an explanation for the direction that plants grow in relation to a light source.
3. Infer an explanation for the different heights of plants grown under varying proportions of light and dark.
4. Infer a relationship between the direction plants grow and the proportion of light they receive.
5. Infer a relationship between starch production in a plant and the plant's reaction to a bromthymol blue solution.
6. Infer an explanation for the similarities and differences in two systems (plant and phenol red solution; animal and phenol red solution) that have been kept in the light for 24 hours.
7. Infer an explanation for the comparison of phenol red solutions placed in the light for 24 hours and in the dark for 24 hours, one system containing plants and the other system containing animals.
8. Make inferences to explain the differences among soaked and unsoaked lima beans, raisins, and prunes.
9. Infer an explanation for the passage of water into a plant.
10. Infer a relationship of plants and animals in an aquarium.
11. Infer an explanation as to why boats float.
12. Infer why all liquids do or do not have the same weight.
13. Make inferences concerning the nature of chemical reactions.
14. Infer factors that might affect the growth of a crystal.
15. Infer the properties of water samples found:
    (a) At the base of a waterfall.
    (b) In a polluted river.
    (c) In the ocean.
    (d) In a stagnant lake.
    (e) In a fast-flowing mountain stream.
16. Make inferences to explain observations of iron filings sprinkled on a piece of paper which is placed on top of a magnet.

17. Infer an explanation for the direction(s) a compass needle points when it is placed in various positions around the magnet.
18. Make inferences to explain observations of iron filings placed on a piece of paper that has a current-carrying wire projecting through the center.
19. Make inferences to explain the direction(s) a compass needle will point when brought close to a wire carrying an electric current.
20. Make inferences to explain the position(s) of (1) iron filings and (2) a compass needle placed on a piece of paper over (1) a single loop of wire carrying an electric current and (2) a coil of wire carrying an electric current.
21. Infer the path taken by electricity to light a flashlight bulb when two wires and one dry cell are used.
22. Infer an explanation for the properties of two lighted flashlight bulbs connected to a dry cell by two, three, and four wires.
23. Infer the location(s) of growth in a tree.
24. Infer from observations of a flower, a function for each of its structures.
25. Make inferences regarding the causes for the characteristics of corn plants.
26. Infer an explanation for the number of colonies of bacteria growing on an inoculated Petri dish.
27. Infer an explanation for the differences in the number of colonies of bacteria on Petri dishes inoculated with various materials.
28. Infer methods of preventing an infection caused by bacteria.
29. Infer an explanation for the similarities and differences of children with their parents.
30. Infer the direction of travel of a beam of light from a bulb.
31. Formulate inferences to explain why objects appear to be of different colors.
32. Infer a reason for the similarities and differences among the spectra of light bulbs, a fluorescent light, and the sun.
33. Infer an explanation for the different spectra produced by chemicals placed in a flame.
34. Infer the advantages of a spectrum over a flame color for the identification of chemicals.
35. Infer a method for measuring the distance between the earth and distant objects, such as the moon, sun, and stars.
36. Infer an explanation for the observed rates of heating and cooling of equal *volumes* of dry and wet white sand, dry and wet dark sand, and water.
37. Formulate inferences to explain the heating and cooling rates of the oceans and the land.
38. Infer an explanation for the formation and development of caves and related structures.

G. Prediction

1. Make predictions regarding the characteristics of plants grown in

G. Prediction *(continued)*

red-green, red-blue, and blue-green light.

2. Make predictions regarding the effect of plants and animals on phenol red solutions after the systems have been in the dark for 24 hours.

3. Predict the similarities of plastic wrap, wax paper, and cellophane with dialysis tubing.

4. Predict the weight of a metal block in air, cooking oil, vinegar, and motor oil.

5. Predict the results of placing a sheet of aluminum foil and a ball of aluminum foil on the surface of a liquid.

6. Predict whether ice will float on alcohol, olive oil, pentane, and turpentine.

7. Predict the temperature, in both Fahrenheit and Celsius units, of various locations outside the classroom.

8. Predict the rate of a chemical reaction when:
    (a) Particle size is changed.
    (b) Concentration is changed.
    (c) Surface area is changed.
    (d) Temperature is changed.

9. Predict the effect on the growth of a crystal by changing the rate of evaporation of the growing solution.

10. Predict the size of one crystal after one month's growth.

11. Predict which compound would produce the largest crystal at the end of a specified period of time.

12. Predict the effects on the growth of a crystal by:
    (a) Adding a second compound to the growing solution.
    (b) Breaking the seed crystal.

13. Predict the effects of neutralized acid and base solutions on litmus paper, and solutions of phenolphthalein, congo red, red cabbage juice, and grape juice.

14. Predict the effects of neutralized acid and base solutions on pieces of marble, zinc, and aluminum.

15. Predict changes that would occur in identical strips of paper placed in a mixture of several different solutions.

16. Predict the direction(s) a compass needle will point when brought close to a wire carrying an electric current.

17. Predict the position(s) of (1) iron filings and (2) a compass needle placed on a piece of paper over (1) a single loop of wire carrying an electric current and (2) a coil of wire carrying an electric current.

18. Predict the way(s) one flashlight bulb, one wire, and a dry cell can be connected so that the bulb will light.

19. Predict the way(s) one flashlight bulb and holder, two wires, and a dry cell can be connected so that the bulb will light.

20. Predict the way(s) two flashlight bulbs, two wires, and a dry cell can be connected so that the bulbs will light.

21. Predict the way(s) one end of a wire can be disconnected causing one and then two flashlight bulbs to go out.

22. Predict the way(s) two flashlight bulbs, three wires, and a dry cell can be connected so that the bulbs will light.
23. Predict the way(s) two flashlight bulbs, four wires, and a dry cell can be connected so that the bulbs will light.
24. Predict the location(s) of growth in the root of a plant.
25. Predict the characteristics of the plants that will germinate from corn seeds.
26. Make predictions regarding the ability of other people to taste the chemical on a piece of PTC paper.
27. Use a graph to predict the area lighted when a bulb is placed at different distances from that area.
28. Predict the color that will be projected on a screen when the screen and the cellophane are the same color.
29. Predict the color to be projected on a screen when the screen and the cellophane are different colors (the screen not being white).
30. Predict the temperature at the end of ten minutes for equal *volumes* of dry and wet white sand, dry and wet dark sand, and water exposed to a heat lamp; and again after it has cooled for ten minutes.
31. Predict the relative heating and cooling rates of equal *weights* of dry and wet white sand, dry and wet dark sand, and water.
32. Predict the relative heating and cooling rates for *mixtures* of half *dry* white sand and half *dry* dark sand in:
    (a) Equal volumes.
    (b) Equal weights.
33. Predict the relative heating and cooling rates for *mixtures* of half *wet* white sand and half *wet* dark sand in:
    (a) Equal volumes.
    (b) Equal weights.
34. Predict the effects of a carbon dioxide solution on marble and limestone.

H. Verification

1. Verify the predictions regarding the characteristics of plants grown in red-green, red-blue, and blue-green light.
2. Verify the presence of starch in the leaves of plants.
3. Verify the presence of carbon dioxide in your breath.
4. Verify the predictions regarding the effect of plants and animals on phenol red solutions after the systems have been in the dark for 24 hours.
5. Verify the predictions of the similarities of plastic wrap, wax paper, and cellophane with dialysis tubing.
6. Verify your predictions concerning the weight of a metal block in air, cooking oil, vinegar, and motor oil.
7. Verify your predictions concerning the results of placing a sheet of aluminum foil and a ball of aluminum foil on the surface of a liquid.
8. Verify the predictions concerning whether ice will float on alcohol, olive oil, pentane, and turpentine.

H. Verification *(continued)*

9. Verify predictions concerning the temperature of various locations outside the classroom.
10. Verify the predictions concerning the rate of a chemical reaction when:
    (a) Particle size is changed.
    (b) Concentration is changed.
    (c) Surface area is changed.
    (d) Temperature is changed.
11. Verify the predictions concerning the effects of neutralized acid and base solutions on litmus paper, and solutions of phenolphthalein, congo red, red cabbage juice, and grape juice.
12. Verify the predictions concerning the effects of neutralized acid and base solutions on pieces of marble, zinc, and aluminum.
13. Verify the predictions concerning the direction(s) a compass needle will point when brought close to a wire carrying an electric current.
14. Verify the predictions concerning the position(s) of (1) iron filings and (2) a compass needle placed on a piece of paper over (1) a single loop of wire carrying an electric current and (2) a coil of wire carrying an electric current.
15. Verify the predictions concerning the way(s) one flashlight bulb, one wire, and one dry cell can be connected so that the bulb will light.
16. Verify the predictions concerning the way(s) one flashlight bulb and holder, two wires, and a dry cell can be connected so that the bulb will light.
17. Verify the predictions concerning the way(s) two flashlight bulbs, two wires, and a dry cell can be connected so that the bulb will light.
18. Verify the predictions concerning the way(s) one end of a wire can be disconnected so that one and then two flashlight bulbs will go out.
19. Verify the predictions concerning the way(s) two flashlight bulbs, three wires, and a dry cell can be connected so that the bulbs will light.
20. Verify the predictions concerning the way(s) two flashlight bulbs, four wires, and a dry cell can be connected so that the bulbs will light.
21. Verify the prediction of the location(s) of growth in the root of a plant.
22. Verify the predictions of the characteristics of the plants that will germinate from corn seeds.
23. Verify the predictions of the area lighted when a bulb is placed at different distances from that area.
24. Verify your predictions concerning the color projected on the screen when the screen and the cellophane are the same color.
25. Verify the predictions concerning the color projected on a screen when the screen and the cellophane are different colors (the screen not being white).
26. Verify the predictions concerning the temperature at the end of ten

minutes of equal *volumes* of dry and wet white sand, dry and wet dark sand, and water exposed to a heat lamp; and then allowed to cool for ten minutes.

27. Verify the prediction concerning the relative heating and cooling rates for equal *weights* of dry and wet white sand, dry and wet dark sand, and water.
28. Verify the predictions concerning the relative heating and cooling rates for mixtures of half dry white sand and half dry dark sand in equal volumes; and in equal weights.
29. Verify the predictions concerning the relative heating and cooling rates for mixtures of half wet white sand and half wet dark sand in equal volumes; and in equal weights.
30. Verify the predictions concerning the effects of a carbon dioxide solution on marble and limestone.

I. Formulation of Hypotheses

1. Formulate hypotheses regarding the differences in the characteristics of plants grown in red, green, and blue light, sunlight, and darkness.
2. Formulate an hypothesis to explain why a bromthymol blue solution changes color when a plant is placed in the solution.
3. Formulate an hypothesis to explain the changes that occur in and around three pieces of dialysis tubing soaked in water: one piece containing sugar and water; one piece containing corn syrup; and the third piece containing water.
4. Formulate hypotheses concerning the abilities of mealworms to see, hear, and smell.
5. Formulate hypotheses concerning the foods that the mealworms prefer to eat.
6. Formulate an hypothesis to explain the changes that occur in an aquarium.
7. Hypothesize reasons for the different temperature readings recorded throughout the classroom.
8. Hypothesize the variables that would affect the rate of motion of a pendulum.
9. Hypothesize the relationship(s) between the behavior of a compass needle and that of a bar magnet.
10. Hypothesize a cause for inconsistent results among classmates concerning the observed properties of two lighted flashlight bulbs.
11. Hypothesize methods of inhibiting the growth of bacteria.
12. Formulate an hypothesis to explain why some students can, and other students cannot, taste the chemical on a piece of PTC paper.
13. Formulate an hypothesis to explain the characteristics of the offspring resulting from the mating of selected fruit flies.

J. Isolation of Variables

1. Isolate the variables that affect the characteristics of plants grown in red, green, and blue light, sunlight, and darkness.

J. Isolation of Variables *(continued)*

2. Isolate the variables that will affect the production of starch in plants.
3. Isolate the variables that will affect a plant's reaction to a bromthymol blue solution.
4. Isolate the variables involved in tests regarding changes in an aquarium.
5. Isolate the variables that affect the weight of different blocks of materials placed in several different liquids.
6. Isolate the variables that might affect the rate of motion of a pendulum.
7. Isolate the variables that caused inconsistencies among the class concerning the observed properties of two lighted bulbs.
8. Isolate the variables that will affect the growth of mold on bread.
9. Isolate the variables that affect the behavior of *Euglena*.

K. Experimentation

1. Plan and conduct an experiment to explain the differences in the characteristics of plants grown in red, green, and blue light, sunlight, and darkness.
2. Plan and conduct an experiment to determine those variables which will affect the production of starch in plants.
3. Plan and conduct an experiment to determine which variables will affect a plant's reaction to a bromthymol blue solution.
4. Plan and conduct an experiment to explain the changes that occur in and around three pieces of dialysis tubing soaked in water: one piece containing sugar and water; one piece containing corn syrup; and the third piece containing water.
5. Plan and conduct experiments to test the hypothesis concerning the ability of mealworms to see, hear, and smell.
6. Plan and conduct experiments to test the hypotheses concerning the foods that mealworms prefer to eat.
7. Plan and conduct an experiment to investigate the causes of changes in an aquarium.
8. Plan and conduct an experiment to determine which variables affect the weight of different blocks of materials placed in several different liquids.
9. Plan and conduct an experiment to determine the effect on the growth of a crystal by changing the state of evaporation of the growing solution.
10. Plan and conduct an experiment to determine the effects on the growth of a crystal by:
    (a) Adding a second compound to the growing solution.
    (b) Breaking the seed crystal.
11. Plan and conduct an experiment, using the identified procedure, to determine the purity of a water sample.
12. Plan and conduct an experiment, using the identified procedure, to purify a water sample.

13. Plan and conduct an experiment, using the identified procedure, to determine whether a substance is an acid.
14. Plan and conduct an experiment, using the identified procedure, to determine which of two acids is the stronger.
15. Plan and conduct an experiment, using the identified procedure, to determine whether an unknown substance is basic.
16. Plan and conduct an experiment, using the identified procedure, to determine which of two basic solutions is the stronger.
17. Plan and conduct an experiment, using the identified procedure, to determine if a solution is neutral.
18. Plan and conduct an experiment to verify the prediction concerning the changes that would occur in identical strips of paper placed in a mixture of several different solutions.
19. Plan and conduct an experiment to test the hypothesis concerning the variables that affect the rate of motion of a pendulum.
20. Plan and conduct an experiment to determine the cause of inconsistent results among the class concerning the observed properties of two lighted bulbs.
21. Plan and conduct an experiment to determine which variables will affect the growth of mold on bread.
22. Plan and conduct an experiment to determine which variables affect the behavior of *Euglena*.
23. Plan and conduct an experiment to determine: (1) environmental conditions that will inhibit the growth of bacteria and (2) chemical substances that will inhibit the growth of bacteria.
24. Plan and conduct an experiment regarding the ability of some students to taste the chemical on a piece of PTC paper.
25. Plan and conduct an experiment to determine the characteristics of the offspring resulting from the mating of selected fruit flies.

APPENDIX Science
EIGHT Content

I. **Current Electricity**
   A. Components of a complete circuit
   B. Parallel and series circuits

II. **Magnetism**
   A. Materials attracted by a magnet
   B. Poles of a magnet
      1. Identification
      2. Characteristics

III. **Magnetic and Electric Fields**
   A. Relation between magnetism and electricity
   B. Strength and shape of magnetic fields
   C. Strength and shape of electric fields

IV. **Measurement**
   A. Distance
   B. Weight
   C. Volume of regular and irregular shaped objects
   D. Heat
   E. Angles
   F. Spherical objects
   G. Time

V. **Density**

VI. **Specific Gravity**

VII. **Light**
   A. Behavior of light rays
   B. Composition of light
   C. Types of spectra

VIII. Growth
  A. Germination of seeds
  B. Growth of plants
     1.   Different parts
     2.   Under varying proportions of light and dark
     3.   Under varying colors of light
  C. Changes occurring in plants and animals during growth
  D. Osmosis
  E. Effects of environment of growth
     1.   Bacteria
     2.   Mold

 IX. Photosynthesis and Respiration
  A. Production of starch in plants
  B. Production of carbon dioxide by plants and animals
  C. Utilization of oxygen by plants and animals
  D. Utilization of carbon dioxide by plants

  X. Reproduction
  A. Function of the parts of the flower
  B. Seeds and germination
  C. Sexual and asexual reproduction in plants and animals

 XI. Genetics
  A. Variations in living organisms due to genetic differences
  B. Dominant and recessive traits
  C. Mendelian ratios

 XII. Life Cycles
  A. Characteristics of the life cycles of plants and animals
  B. Cells
  C. Bacteria
  D. Mold

XIII. Ecology: plant and animal relationships in an aquarium

XIV. Energy
  A. Heat transfer
  B. Heat absorption

 XV. Properties of materials
  A. Physical
  B. Chemical

XVI. Minerals
  A. Properties
  B. Cave formation

XVII. Water
A. Hard and soft
B. Other impurities
C. Purification

XVIII. Solutions
A. Types
B. Crystals
1. Properties
2. Growth

XIX. Chemical Reactions
A. Types
B. Effect on the rate of:
1. Particle size of reactants
2. Concentration of reactants
3. Surface area of reactants
4. Temperature of reactants

XX. Chromatography
A. Effects of different paper
B. As a separation technique
C. As an identification technique

XXI. Acids and Acidic Properties
A. Physical properties
B. Reaction with indicators
C. Reaction with minerals
D. Reaction with metals
E. Strengths

XXII. Bases and Basic Properties
A. Physical properties
B. Reaction with indicators
C. Reaction with minerals
D. Reaction with metals
E. Reaction with fats and oils
F. Strengths

XXIII. Neutralization and Neutrality
A. Effects of mixing acids and bases
B. Reaction with indicators
C. Reaction with minerals
D. Reaction with metals
E. Test for neutrality

2 3 4 5 6 7 8 9 10